Postured for Power
Team Edition

30 Spiritual Adjustments for Kingdom Teams

Andrew T. Arroyo

Postured For Power Team Edition
by Andrew T. Arroyo

Printed in the United States of America

ISBN 1-594677-50-6

www.xulonpress.com

Table of Contents

To

My fellow team members past, present, future

You are brave and wise souls.

Acknowledgements and Author's Note

Nearly one full year after publishing the original *Postured for Power*, a new vision has sprouted in my heart. It is a vision for a series of *Postured for Power* books based on this well-received theme.

Postured for Power Team Edition is the logical choice to lead off. Once we've dealt with our personal leadership posture, it makes sense to deal with the posture we take in coming together. The same five spiritual postures required for leadership power are required for team power—only the insights and applications are different.

Personalize what you read here. Make it about your team. Resist the urge to categorize this as a church book. Teams come in all shapes and shades—sports, business, ministry, military, and even the family unit—and *God's desire is that every team formed in his name prospers!* Whatever type of team you serve on, this team edition of Postured for Power will guide you and your teammates to great heights.

Even as I write this sentence I am just four days away from back surgery. The homebound period is estimated at four weeks, so I intend to write the majority of this book while on my back. Meanwhile, guess what will happen to my church and other endeavors? Do you think they will crumble at my absence? Will all spill into chaos? Need I rush my recovery to get back in the saddle? The answer is none of the above. The reason for the answer is team!

I believe in team. I have resolved to do nothing if not through a team. The majority of my energies are poured into developing teams that are, as the saying goes, greater than the sum of their parts. Past investment in teams yields me this present luxury of peace as I head into surgery. Not only will things not fall apart in my absence, but they will grow!

So, it is with great thanks that I acknowledge the teams I serve with and on. You know who you are. Because of you, everything God has set before us is more than probable…it is possible!

Thanks to my wife, Katie, for again proofing the manuscript. Carlton McLeod, friend and colleague lent his encouragement to the project. David Arroyo has stepped up his leadership during this time, proving again the importance of team. Friends and fellow co-laborers in our quest to plant House Churches also deserve mention—Cedric and Anna Bobb, Chris and Rebecca Henderson, Becky Charron, Tony Morgan, John and Barbara Williams, Chuck Krueger, and Jacque King. And my pastor, Bobby Hill, deserves credit for helping me with that special something called "focus."

We are headed somewhere good together. Onward and upward we go.

Andrew T. Arroyo
Norfolk, VA
May 2004

Introduction

The power of one?

Five spiritual postures are necessary for Kingdom power. The postures derive from 1 Peter 5:5-10, and include humility, relinquishment, separation, defense, and resolution. Note the postures in Peter's language:

> *(**Humility**)...and all of you, clothe yourselves with humility toward one another, for God is opposed to the proud, but gives grace to the humble. Humble yourselves, therefore, under the mighty hand of God, that He may exalt you at the proper time, (**Relinquishment**) casting all your anxiety upon Him, because He cares for you. (**Separation**) Be of sober spirit, be on the alert. (**Defense**) Your adversary, the devil, prowls about like a roaring lion, seeking someone to devour. But resist him, (**Resolution**) Firm in your faith, knowing that the same experiences of suffering are being accomplished by your brethren who are*

> *in the world. And after you have suffered a little while, the God of all grace, who called you to His eternal glory in Christ, will Himself perfect, confirm, strengthen and establish you.*

In the first *Postured for Power* edition, we looked at these postures through the lens of Kingdom leadership. As for this present edition, we build upon the previous foundation and turn our attention to Kingdom teams. This book is a tour through the five postures as they relate to Kingdom teams. Call it a thirty-day spiritual workout for your team.

Hunker down, soldiers of God. The Kingdom challenge about Kingdom work taking place through Kingdom teams is here. The blueprint for positioning and baptizing your Kingdom teams in Kingdom power so you can become a brute force to be reckoned with is before you. This book is that challenge and call. You and your team are going to be put through some serious adjustments in preparation to be that force. Whether your team is for ministry, business, sports, military, or another endeavor, *Postured for Power Team Edition* is designed for you.

This month could change the destiny and dynamic of your team. This month *will* change your team! I am as eager as you to begin, but first let's make the case for the value of teams and the need for empowerment through right posture.

The power of one

The case for teams is easy to make. The power

of one is a farce. I'll take your "one" and raise you by a "team" any day—and if my team is properly postured for the power of God, it will outdo anything you can accomplish alone. Las Vegas offers no comparable odds. The win is guaranteed. The notion that one is anything but the loneliest, puniest—and weakest—number is false.

Of course, this idea of teams trumping individuality is unpopular in our postmodern times. A prime example is a recent ad campaign I witnessed.

I could not believe my eyes and ears. Is a branch of the United States Armed Forces actually touting itself on national television as the perfect avenue for individual accomplishment? As surely as I was sitting on my couch watching their latest commercial, they were doing just that. Targeting the naïve and naturally selfish demographic of eighteen to twenty-four year old males, they were peddling a pack of lies.

Now, I'm wise to the system. Promotion and rank is based on individual merit. The military does offer motivated individuals an opportunity to shine, and rightly so if they have the stuff. I also know that a great many military people are in it for themselves. Nonetheless, I would like to see a single member of the military—from private to general—take on another army alone. Point made. I've heard of one-man-bands, but never of a one-man-army. And if that's what a would-be soldier aims to become, then the result is not powerful it's pitiful!

Maybe it's just me, but if I'm in the trenches next to you, and I discover your prime reason for enlisting was self-actualization, then I might seek someone else to fight alongside. With the battle raging, if you're thinking about "how can I maximize myself like that commercial said I could," then you've taken a wrong turn somewhere, my friend. Go ahead and earn your medal, but on someone else. I am here to achieve our objective as a unit, because I know first-hand my own inadequacies in achieving something "this big" on my own. In the military, as in any team, the whole is truly more than the sum of its parts.

Without speaking for you, let me declare here and now that I need a team. If that makes me a wimp, then so be it. No amount of personal gusto substitutes for a solid team. Do not believe the lie that you can or should tackle any challenge on your lonesome. Wherever possible, make it happen with a team. Except in extraordinary circumstances when you must approach a situation alone, the preliminary decision to team up is an important step toward power.

Know this. God *uses* teams. Groups are his preferred artillery for brokering Kingdom wins. Through our interdependence the work of God is done.

Universal principle

Teams are part of a larger universal principle: Nothing happens in isolation. Interdependence rather than independence underlies every activity without exception. This is a matter of natural law touching every cell and fiber of creation.

We could illustrate this fact through detailed scientific data, but that is not necessary. Our own bodies are example enough. The human body is the most brilliant picture we have of interdependence and teamwork, and of the preference of God to do things through groups rather than unilateral motion.

Watch your body at work. No body part stands alone. Each part works together, at once pushing or pulling, acting or reacting, in fluid (unified!) motion toward a singular goal. Even the simplest act of moving fork to mouth requires teamwork within the body. The body parts never wait to function together until the really big tasks, like climbing a mountain or moving a heavy box. In sleep mode and awake, in large tasks and in small, the body operates smoothly and consistently in team-like fashion.

This is how God would like Kingdom people to work. "Now you are Christ's body, and individually members of it" (1 Cor. 12:27). You saw that verse coming a mile away. If you are not a church team, do not shut your heart to the revelation. You do not have to be a church team to be Christ's extension; you only have to be committed to Kingdom purposes. Kingdom purposes can range from doing business God's way to educating in a sound manner to reclaiming a violence-infested community.

As the human body functions through interdependent reliance between its parts, so ought Kingdom teams function through people working together. "For the body is not one member, but many" (v. 14).

Power link

Do you get how important teams are? If you do

get it, then you are ready for the second half of the revelation: Power is available in superabundance for Kingdom teams, far more so than for Kingdom individuals.

Paul continues, writing, "If they were all one member, where would the body be? (v. 19)." In other words, Paul asks, "How can a single individual even compare with a group?" There is no comparison! Coming together is a key link to the power of God.

Yet coming together is not the only link. It is a start, but not the end. Power is not promised just for coming together. If it were, many more teams (and churches) would be much more powerful! In actuality, one more ingredient is needed: Posture.

The idea behind these daily posture adjustments is simple. Even as physical posture is critical for power in athletics, so is spiritual posture for Kingdom power. In order to flow in increasing measures of the power, the spiritual posture of the team or group must be in good alignment. I submit that God empowers teams more than individuals, but not just any team. He empowers the team that is properly postured. If spiritual posture is important for individuals, then how much more important is it for teams?

We can all agree that an impotent team is not worth forming, and certainly not worth continuing. Power is needed for success. God needs Kingdom teams that are potent and powerful enough to carry out his purposes with excellence and fullness. Sadly, a great many teams run at quarter power without knowing it. Some know it and do not care. Many are too lazy to attend to their personal posture, let alone the corporate side. Which type of team is yours?

On that note, let's begin our month together. For more on the link between posture and power, I direct you to the Introduction of the first edition, as it is foundational to this entire series. If you have grasped the connection already, we can proceed immediately to the Posture of Humility and Day One.

I

Posture of

Humility

...and all of you, clothe yourselves with
humility toward one another,
for God is opposed to the proud,
but gives grace to the humble.
Humble yourselves, therefore, under the mighty
hand of God, that He may exalt you
at the proper time.
1 Peter 5:5-6

Day 1
Humility Adjustment

Who's in charge?

(Upward Humility)

Nine out of ten people will think this question when joining a new team. Every tenth person might actually break the silence and ask it. The question is this: "Who's in charge here?"

The gentle warning of today's team adjustment is to make God king of your team. Young and old, experienced or not, we are his subjects. Let us humble ourselves under his mighty hand and no other. Either he is in charge, or we charge in alone.

Meet the boss

We are talking about Christian teams, aren't we? If so, then it is appropriate to establish the foundation upon which every godly team rests: The foundation of the Triune God himself—Father, Son, and Holy Spirit. God is the boss of your team!

And he is Captain, if your team is for sports.

And he is Senior Pastor, if your team is for church.

And he is Commander-in-Chief, if your team is for the military.

And he is Superintendent and Dean, if your team is for education.

And he is General Sales Manager, if your team is for marketing.

And he is Web Master, if your team is for cyber development.

And he is Chair, if your team is a board of directors...whatever your team or organization, the ultimate leader must be God if it would be postured for power.

Paul drives this home: "He is before all things, and in Him all things hold together. He is also head of the body" (Col. 1:17-18a). The beginning. The end. The all in all. The be all and end all. He is God. Let no man on your team usurp the authority and rule of God. The producer of the show, he first is in charge.

Team pride

Pride is a real and present danger for teams. Individuals are not pride's sole targets. Pride tows the coastline like a pirate ship, and it will happily take down whatever vessel comes its way. Whether you are alone on a dingy, or with a dozen people on a yacht, pride schemes to climb aboard and assume control. Given the choice, he will always overthrow the larger vessel carrying the most people. He wants numbers, so your team is a target.

Yes, team pride exists, and it is just as cancerous to Kingdom work as individual pride. Given its way, pride hands God his walking papers and puts man in charge. Teams that operate in pride have decided that the power of the many is greater—or at least more desirable—than the power of the One. Members collectively block out God with their own agendas and visions, and fight with one another to assume control of the helm to steer the ship where they want it to go. It is Babel all over again. "Come, let us build for ourselves a city…let us make for ourselves a name" (Gen. 11:4).

Of course, there is a difference between having positive team spirit and sinful team pride. God is for team spirit—the corporate feeling of oneness and dogged tenacity to emerge victorious over the competition, coupled with the healthy belief that such is possible. It is the team that crosses the line from spirit to pride that God hates. The difference is that the prideful team not only thinks positively about its capacity, but believes that it is inherently better—more righteous, more able, more invulnerable—than other teams.

"Impossible," you say, "There is no way any team I serve on can become so prideful. We love God, we have a humble view of ourselves. We exist to serve him even if we don't say it every time we meet."

But I beg to differ. The very thing one says is impossible is actually the very thing that is most possible. The moment you label this or that pitfall "impossible" is the moment we develop our first blind spot. A single blind spot, my dear friends, is all the devil needs to bring your team down. Just one is all it takes.

So don't delay. Swing widely around and cast a broad floodlight on this area. Fire up that lighthouse and scan the coast for pirates. When next you come together as a team, make haste to re-affirm who is in charge of this team. Exalt the lordship of Christ. Do so as one man with one mind (Acts 1:14). Posture your selves as humble servants of the Most High God. This is step one in being clothed with power of a brand you have never known.

Hail to the chief

Acknowledging God as your chief is a matter of humility. Unless your team breaks the mold, humility of this sort requires continuous attention to maintain. Part of the humility maintenance program is having frequent times of corporate yielding to God. You need to hail the chief together on a regular basis!

Adjust your posture in such a way as to salute and affirm his position in your midst. Testify of his greatness. Observe his hand in bringing you together. Recall the storms he has carried you through. Recount your shared HIS-story. Marvel at the diversity of your team, and how he has implanted a uniquely valid contribution in each member. Gaze at the future like Abraham gazed at the stars. Stand awe-struck before your God; and do this *together*.

Join hands. Lift holy hands. Kneel on the beach like Paul with the Ephesian elders. Prostrate your bodies on the ground. Just worship your God and give him the place of primacy always. This is the posture of humility. It is through this upward attention that upward power flows.

Never should too much time pass before you assemble at the altar in this humble posture. The altar can be a huddle, a board table, a water cooler, a locker room, or a campfire for all God cares. Physical location is not important; spiritual location is. Let the spiritual location of your team be fixed humbly in God. Incorporating regular prayer, worship, reflection, and declaration of who is really in charge into your team meetings will keep God on top, humility in play, and pride at bay.

Day 2
Humility Adjustment

Slave, salve

(Outward Humility)

Slave is the word of the hour for God-fearing believers worldwide. Through humble armies of the slaves of God, healing is delivered daily to the world's doorstep.

Think about it. Slaves are God's salves. (The letters spelling "slave" also spell "salve" when rearranged.) A salve is a healing ointment, bringing relief and cure wherever it is spread. This is what your team becomes when it chooses the position of slave. You become a salve applied strategically to your corner of the world. Your team should posture itself for radically humble service of this sort.

Always in style

With every change of season, Paris introduces a change in fashion. Many consumers bite, and spend billions to ride the crest of the trend. But for the believer, spiritual style should never change. Slavery is always in fashion. Jesus wove the pattern: "(But) whoever wishes to become great among you shall be your servant; and whoever wishes to be first among you shall be slave of all" (Mk. 10:43-44).

Oh, what thunderous power is locked up in that

tiny term! *Slave*! Imagine the new meaning your life would take on if you daily dressed in the spiritual garments of a slave and nothing more. Now go one step further. Imagine your team suited in slave dress alone. Not as multiple slaves with divergent agendas and royal robes concealed beneath, but so joined in perfect unity as to be one under God for the world? What power, what authentic spiritual authority, what healing balm would be loosed into your land.

***The* measure**

Have you ever sat down to ponder the value of your team? In your calculations, be sure to factor in the degree to which your team is a slave. Your outward humility in service is the measure of your value.

Jesus exclaimed, "...but if the salt has become tasteless...it is good for nothing anymore, except to be thrown out and trampled under foot by men" (Matt. 5:13). Could it be said also that if a team ceases to bring good repair through its humble efforts—if it loses its salve-ness, if you will—then it too is good for nothing?

Life as a Kingdom team exists for one over-arching purpose, to serve. This is what slaves do. They serve. The measure of your team's value is, quite plainly, how well it serves the purposes of God as a slave-salve of God.

Do not paint me as hyper-spiritual. Other measures of value are important. Sports teams have stats and scores; business teams have profit and loss statements; military teams have body counts and redrawn maps showing ground taken; ministry teams have souls saved and discipled into maturity. Tangible results are necessary, or the team is a waste of time. Yet the ultimate system of measure is whether your team is a slave—first, last, and everywhere in between.

What this means

This posture starts with attitude. An early Christian hymn put it something like this: "Have this attitude in yourselves which was also in Christ Jesus, who, although He existed in the form of God, did not regard equality with God a thing to be grasped, but emptied Himself, taking the form of a bond-servant" (Phil. 2:5-7). So this involves, in part, going through an attitude adjustment to move from self to slave. It all boils down to humility.

How this applies in practical terms is up to you. At the most superficial level it means your team is an agent of good rather than harm. At deeper levels it means your team is active in lovingly extending the Kingdom into the hearts of people.

Can a military unit with its bullets and bombs be a slave? Yes, by avoiding senseless murder and malice even as it carries out its job, and by participating in the re-building of countries it penetrates rather than subjecting and tearing down.

Can a basketball team with its need to be aggressive and goal-oriented (literally) be a slave? Yes, by its attitude toward the referees, the fans, and the other team, and by service projects it engages in off the court. Not to mention by how you treat your fellow teammates, and how they treat you.

Can a guerilla negotiation company with its stiff bottom lines and take-no-prisoners mandate be a slave? Yes, by refraining from unethical practices and outright lies, and by negotiating only for that which holds promise to help rather than hurt others.

Can *your* team attain results and still be a slave? You can if you want to. Anything is possible for the willing. Get creative. Color outside the lines. You are without excuse.

Irony

The irony of today's adjustment is not lost on me. Everything in this adjustment is teeming with paradox. Of course, you probably know that the Kingdom is full of great ironies. Chief among them is this idea of slavery.

Under carnal circumstances we think of slavery in terms of bondage, ignorance, and heaped insult—not to mention abject weakness. It is a very dehumanizing term with ugly connotations. Yet in Kingdom-speak, slave means just the opposite.

In God's economy the slave is celebrated. You are not "just a slave." You can wear the title, ironically, with godly pride. It is your badge. Exaltation is the prized fate of all who endure humiliation for Christ as slaves, for all who choose to do the right thing. I daresay every team that chooses the slave mantle will share the same prized fate, both in the life to come and in this life on earth.

The key to attaining the prize is a pact between you and your fellow members to hold fast to service as slaves. The slave posture is one of humility that is easy to assume in the beginning, but very difficult to hold until the end. Many a team has formed under the guise of Kingdom work, only to cross the finish line having long since traded their slave clothes for the garments of fleshly royalty.

My concern is that your team finishes as it began—as a slave to the purposes of the Kingdom. May whatsoever fervor for service that drove your team initially intensify with time rather than diminish. May your team be able to make Paul's dying words your own, declaring, "For I am already being poured out as a drink offering...I have fought the good fight, I have finished the course, I have kept the faith" (2 Tim. 4:6-7).

But for that to happen, your team must bend to a slave posture and remain there stubbornly. You must pursue the slave posture, positioning yourselves outwardly as humble servants. Slavery is one posture worth guarding with your lives.

Day 3
Humility Adjustment

Competition

(Outward Humility)

Most teams compete on one level or another. Business to business, sport to sport—whether the prize is the thrill of victory or something more substantial, competition is the road there. Two teams slug it out, with one left standing a bit higher than the other.

Even ministry teams compete. I encourage teams I oversee to out-do one another in loving, serving, and excellence. Good-spirited competition helps all of us to keep sharp and goal-oriented. Competition is the antidote to stagnation.

Your team probably competes on some level too. Much of what teams do can be classified as competition. The struggle is to maintain a humble posture. Somehow, win, lose, or draw, humility must be the display of the day.

Good or bad

Self-styled peace lovers rail against competition. They would like to throw out letter grades in school; do away with point systems in games; force the wealthy to redistribute to the less-than-wealthy; and erase every record from the books so no one feels bad when encountering feats they have no hope to beat. Listen to their stump speech long enough and you will begin believing competition is of the devil himself, and that winners are the biggest losers of all. But is that true?

No! The problem lies not with competition, but with competitors. Rather, the trouble lies in the competitors. Poor sports are so because of pride.

Competition is good if conducted with humility. Your team should be encouraged to go for the gusto in competition. Shoot for nothing less than gold. Aim for the bull's eye. Never throw the game, set, or match from a feeling that winning is sin. Only win and celebrate the victory from a posture of humility.

Our usual posture

Humility in competition is easier said than done, as this childhood illustration shows. Hot, sweaty, and tired, the two small town soccer teams formed single file lines after the game. According to tradition, the ranks were to walk past each other to slap hands and say, "Good game (slap), good game (slap), good game (slap)...". The trouble was that we were nine and ten year olds; and our concern was less with being good sports and more with getting our last dig into the other team before going home.

So we spit on our hands. That way every "good game (slap)" interaction carried an unexpected, and unwanted, wet surprise. Whether we won or lost did not matter. If we won, the spit signified that the other team was beneath us. If we lost, it signified that we were too cool to care. They would get theirs at last.

It's a good thing those days are over. We have moved beyond such childish ways. Or have we? I am not so sure. Adults too display competitive pride, only by means of greater complexity and insidiousness!

Truth be told, our default posture before, during, and after competition is pride. This means we need some work to display humility regardless of what happens.

Humility in victory

Victory puffs up. Maybe not one or two victories; but over time, if your team is so good that securing victory becomes like second nature, then some degree of puffiness is to be expected. Since pride comes before a fall, you had best learn some humility in your victory and fast!

I offer two suggestions. First, always have a divine pin handy. A pin is useful for popping ballooned egos. Scripture is the best pin. Locate a handful of verses that you can read after every victory to give eternal perspective and to put you back in your place. Job has some of the best: "Now gird up your loins like a man, and I will ask you...Where were you when I laid the foundation of the earth? Have you ever in your life commanded the morning, and caused the dawn to know its place? Can you bind the chains of Pleiades, or loose the cords of Orion? Do you know the ordinances of the heavens, or fix their rule over the earth?" (Job 38:3, 4, 12, 31, 33). If this does not burst your bubble, nothing will!

Second, if you must boast, boast in the Lord. Jeremiah wrote, "Let not a wise man boast of his wisdom, and let not the mighty man boast of his might, let not a rich man boast of his riches; but let him who boasts boast of this, that he understands and knows me, that I am the LORD who exercises lovingkindness, justice, and righteousness on earth" (Jer. 9:23-24). In other words, use the platform afforded by your victory as an opportunity to declare the awesome nature of God to all who listen. Imagine an entire team acting this way!

Humility in defeat

But then there is defeat. Sometimes I wonder if it isn't easier to be humble in victory than in defeat. Sure, defeat is humiliating, but humiliation is no guarantee of humility. Defeat is a blow to the ego. But unless the ego is pliable and willing to bend into a posture of humility, the natural tendency of the ego is to harden up and push back.

Excuses are one way we harden up and push back. Heaven forbid we congratulate the other team. No, we blame our defeat on any number of reasons other than the victors. We failed to gel, they cheated, or it was a fluke—it could not have been that they were better. If an excuse can be found, we will make use of it. This is pride.

Humility in defeat displays no ego. It has a secure and godly identity, but it has no ego. Learn the difference between godly identity and ego. The perfect time is after your next defeat, when you feel ego rising up in carnal self-defense. God will make these principles clearer to you at that time if you have ears to hear.

On display

In final analysis, your team is on display before the world. "Because we have become a spectacle to the world, both to angels and to men" (1 Cor. 4:9). How you carry yourselves in victory and in defeat is a key factor in how high God chooses to raise you up.

Like trophies in a case, the most impressive are given the place of prominence. If you are content for God to display your team on a lower rung or hidden on a cluttered shelf, then neglect humility in competition. But if you desire a prime place of display, then posture your team in humility no matter how the competition shakes out. God delights in such ones!

Humble in victory; gracious in defeat. This is the motto of a godly team. These are the trophies of heaven!

Day 4
Humility Adjustment

Friction

(Inward Humility)

Let's review. The humility adjustment on day one had to do with *upward* humility—the relation of your team toward God. The second and third adjustments had to do with *outward* humility—the relation of your team toward the world around us. The final two humility adjustments will turn us *inward*—to the relation of your team members one to another.

The heat is on! Let us hope humility is too.

Friction

Today's adjustment deals with inward friction. Have you ever experienced friction with a team member, or witnessed friction between your teammates? Sure you have.

Where does the friction come from? Immediately we might be tempted to answer, "Pride!" But that is not necessarily the case. To be sure, usually it comes from team members butting heads. That does not signal pride though. Like two hands rubbed together vigorously, friction is the natural byproduct of two or more individuals passionately pursuing a given outcome. Under this definition, humble people experience friction too!

The result of the friction can be very good when humble people are involved. The more friction your team is willing to endure, the more barriers your team will break. The more barriers your team can break, the more likely it is to achieve success. If this were a book on how to conduct meetings, I would advise every member of your team to take a no-holds-barred approach each time you meet. Let the feathers fly. Allow friction to develop, test ideas, disagree about maneuvers and strategies, dole every suggestion a healthy beating to see if it holds up to scrutiny.

Friction is good. Only make sure that the process is defined by inward, member-to-member humility. A team that masters high friction with inward humility is a force to be reckoned with.

How high = how much

How much friction does your team have to endure? The answer is directly proportional to how high your team wishes to go. Does your team shoot for the mediocre or the majestic? Are you content with an in-field bunt or is the back fence and emptied bases the goal? Is success defined by a barely passing grade or is true excellence your mission? You see, greatness requires quite a climb, causing much friction on the way.

Teams that achieve great things do not arrive there smoothly. Because the road to excellence is bumpy and windy, and because high amounts of activity are required to pull off that project, game, or task with precision, friction is to be expected. Lesser teams immaturely hope for the yellow brick road (as in "easy path"); but they are quickly surprised and splintered when friction appears from nowhere. They hoped for the country club but they got the farm.

I am here to tell you to fear not—friction is natural! Do not be taken off guard when it comes. As long as your friction is humble friction, you will get through.

Humble friction

Humble friction? It seems impossible, but I assure you it is not. The key is in how you approach it in the heat of the moment. Do you approach it like a viper, striking back and forth aiming to kill? Do you lock horns and attempt to gore the other to show who is boss? Do you play Devil's advocate better than the old snake himself? Well then, the mystery of why your team is falling apart is solved. No need to hire a high-priced consultant or pay a prophet to perceive the problem. Pride has gotten into your team, and the friction that began as a positive is about to bring down the house. You need to inject humility into that team of yours, and fast.

The key to positive friction is humility. Humility is an issue of tenor and timeliness. Look carefully at this admonition: "Let no unwholesome word proceed from your mouth, but only such a word as is good for edification according to the need of the moment, that it may give grace to those who hear" (Eph. 4:29). The tenor of every verbal exchange should be positive even when questioning a position or forcing a clarification. Remember, the arrow should be aimed at the idea, not the other person.

And the timeliness of every verbal exchange likewise should be appropriate. Questioning and creating friction just for its own sake is a losers' game.

Put aside inward rivalries. "Let all bitterness and wrath and anger and clamor and slander be put away from you, along with all malice. And be kind to one another, tender-hearted, forgiving each other, just as God in Christ also has forgiven you" (4:31-32). This is the way to humble friction.

The best part

Now to the best part. When you engage in humble friction, something heavenly transpires. Literally, heavenly.

First, God's will is done, resulting in the best possible output from your team. This is cause for celebration, because God's Kingdom has been extended yet again through you his agents.

Second, God shows up in a very special way as the oil of the Holy Spirit. The Holy Spirit is the oil that preserves the unity you have been striving for. High-friction teams require high viscosity oil to maintain smooth operation. Even the largest dose of man's humility is not enough to keep the machine functioning smoothly for long. (All the honest people said, "Amen!") You need a grade of oil viscous enough to handle Kingdom friction routinely. *The only such oil I know of is the oil of the Holy Spirit.*

Gladly, he is all the willing to lube Kingdom teams. Those teams that dare to tow the red line are the ones that most attract him. He gets bored with teams that play it safe. Edgy teams are his style. Just mix in the right amount of humility, and color him there. "Behold, how good and how pleasant it is for brothers to dwell together in unity! It is like the precious oil upon the head, coming down upon the beard, even Aaron's beard, coming down upon the edge of his robes" (Ps. 133:1-2).

Day 5
Humility Adjustment

No glory

(Inward Humility)

You need two doses of humility for today's adjustment: one to get through the reading, the other to apply it. Between you and me, I do not expect that everyone is going to get it the first time around.

This adjustment contains some ideas that are difficult to swallow, perhaps that are even offensive. One might easily argue that these ideas are petty, whereas really they are precise. The changes this adjustment calls for fall into the precision category. There is a difference. Some adjustments are life or death, while others target the finer points. This falls into the latter.

Suspend your judgments, and see if the Holy Spirit comes through with even a kernel of truth. I suspect he will. First we will unpack the general problem, then we will discuss how teams can help solve it.

The problem

First, let's set up the general problem. Everyone has heard it; many have said it. After giving a good performance someone approaches you with congratulations. Then, in knee-jerk stereotypical fashion, you dodge the compliment saying, "It wasn't me, it was God." For effect, you might even jut your index finger toward the sky.

Not *that* good

A wise woman once said to me the next time someone replies to my compliment by saying, "It wasn't me, it was God," remark back, saying, "Gee, I hope not. It wasn't all that good!"

Ouch! We're friends here, aren't we? A comment like that hurts so good. You get the point. If it really were "all God" who sang that song, or played that game, or delivered that sermon or sales pitch, it would have turned out a whole lot better than it did. Even on our best day we could never in a zillion years be as God in all his glory and splendor.

Be truthful. Nothing you and your team do is so good that God should get the sole credit. To be sure, he must get the sole glory. But the sole credit? That is another story.

There is a difference between credit and glory. You can get credit and still give glory to God. Credit is what one receives for having a key role and making a good effort. Glory is what one receives for the changes that result from the effort.

Did you put in the time? Did you give it your all? Then receive the compliment, take credit, say thank you, and move on. Receiving credit does not automatically make you prideful. What makes you prideful is when you act like it was nothing, but deep inside you know it was anything but.

False humility

The "it's not me, it's God" phrase is really just another form of pride. Or, if you prefer, we can call it false humility. How so? True humility seeks no glory, but it does not shirk from receiving due credit. False humility on the other hand seeks no credit, but secretly wants all the glory. In a weird way, the act of bouncing the credit to God allows our flesh to receive glory.

Let me illustrate how this false humility works. If you compliment me on a job well done, then I want to make sure you know that GOD himself—as though in the flesh—has seen fit to incarnate me and use me to deliver the purest of the pure performance to you, the lesser. I want you to know that GOD has chosen me, "just" a servant, to rock your world. I want you to believe that what you just received from me was so pure and perfect that you should never forget it, and that you were blessed to have had such a vessel of honor in your presence. So I give God the credit for the performance you just witnessed; while I keep the glory for being so totally usable in the Potter's hands. No matter if later that day or night I sit before God to share some of the glory, because of my actions of false humility I have already robbed both him and me of our rightful due.

In contrast, true humility does the following. If you compliment me on a job well done, then some credit is due me. I practiced, I prepared, I showed up, I was faithful, I prayed, and I executed my task with excellence. Therefore, I should receive positive credit for doing my part and doing it right. If I possess true humility, then I respond to you by simply saying, "Thank you. I am blessed that you were blessed."

With true humility, there is no need to flail about in the moment in some vain effort to look super-spiritual. Later that day or evening, after I am alone with God, I can bow before his throne, thank him for using me, and release glory to him. *All of it. In private.* That way I have received the credit I was due, God has received all the glory, and the person who offered the compliment was allowed to go about his or her way without having to put up with my antics.

Team steps in

This is where the benefit of being part of a team steps in. You can keep one another grounded. With the right posture of humility, you can make sure fellow teammates get due credit, while God gets all the glory—and you can hold one another accountable to avoid foolish shows of false humility.

It begins by making a pact that false humility shall no longer have a place in your group. Should false humility appear, speedy confrontation must ensue. Agreement on this point is non-negotiable. If I see it in you, then I am bound by our pact to confront it. Vice versa if you see it in me.

You also must encourage one another to receive credit graciously. In other words, saying thank you in response to a compliment is just plain good manners—and like all proper etiquette, it should be normal practice for every member. If you have some particularly crass members who are so ingrained against receiving due credit gracefully, then you will need to practice with them how to do it. Over and over and over again, you must practice this until they get it.

Finally, you must instill in every member what it means to give the glory to God. Do we really think giving God the glory is done with a few words and an upward-pointing index finger? Rather, giving God the glory for the fruit of one's labor is a very intimate endeavor. It occurs in that secret place when no one is looking. "Beware of practicing your righteousness before men to be noticed by them…But you, when you pray, go into your inner room, and when you have shut your door, pray to your Father who is in secret, and your Father who sees in secret will repay you." (Matt. 6:1, 6)

For me, the act of giving God the glory is so private that I will not even share what I say and do in that moment. If you hear me speak or read my books and wish to compliment me, then I will be gracious to you. I will say, "Thank you." I will receive the credit you so ascribe, humbly. But you will not be privy to the conversation with God I will have later that day, wherein I give him the glory. This is reserved for his ears alone.

You will have to find your own way. Just avoid the delusion that dodging compliments makes you humble. A team that learns to take credit but give glory is a team postured for power.

II

Posture of Relinquishment

...casting all your anxiety upon Him,
because He cares for you.
1 Peter 5:7

Day 6
Relinquishment Adjustment

Fresh start

We humans are interesting creatures. We are pack rats—collecting and holding the miscellaneous. Be it in a junk drawer, a closet, or a garage, we have stuff. What it does other than clutter walkways we do not know, but we keep it anyway.

The same is true spiritually and emotionally. We are packrats. Memories and experiences—especially bad ones—stand floor to ceiling in our psyche. Some of this stockpiling is good for memorializing mistakes we do not wish to repeat. Most of it, like scar tissue, hinders us from moving forward, especially when forming new teams and working relationships.

Let's take some time over the next few days to put some of our clutter on the lawn. The ability to relinquish at least some of the past impacts your ability to enter the future with your team. Cast it all on him. He cares that you get a fresh start.

Past is dead

In eight of the most stunning words ever spoken, Jesus challenged a man, saying, "Allow the dead to bury their own dead" (Lk. 9:60). What did he mean?

The translation is simple: The past is the past. What once was is no more. Cast the memory into the deep. Relinquish it and let it go. Make a fresh start and follow me today. The day deserves a fair shake.

Each new Kingdom team deserves a fair shake from every member, regardless of past bad experiences. For every member of a team, there is a corresponding history. I have a history, and you have a history. The extent to which we allow our history to color our expectations for the future is a key determinant in how far we can go together. If I expect that the same negativity from a past team will infect our current team, then guess what? It will.

The experience of new beginnings requires relinquishment of past histories. The posture of relinquishment helps us experience the joy of new beginnings.

Prejudice

Do you want new beginnings? Then relinquish your memories. Unrelinquished memories produce prejudice, which is the enemy of new beginnings.

Consider a middle-aged woman who is three times divorced. Each divorce was the result of a cheating husband. We would all agree that those men did her wrong. But does that mean that all men are cheaters and would do her wrong? Would it be fair for this woman to prejudge every man she meets as a cheater-waiting-to-happen? Of course not! Yet how many women with similar experiences do just that, becoming cynical toward men and skeptical of women who claim to have faithful men? I tell you the truth; they will never find a good man with that attitude.

Consider now a man who has served on ten teams in the last fifteen years. Six were business teams, two were church teams, one was a community anti-crime task force, and one was a softball team that he joined just for fun. Seven of the ten teams were sour experiences. The reasons why are unimportant. What is important is his memory of those sour experiences and whether he allows them to influence his prejudgment of future teams he might join.

If he is typical, the seven negative experiences will overshadow the three positives. Like the woman with the anti-male chip on her shoulder, he will likely be unenthusiastic about future teams. The sad ending to the story is that, just like the woman whose bitterness toward men makes finding a good man unlikely, so does this man's distaste for teams make becoming part of a truly great team equally unlikely. His predisposed attitude seals his fate. And the spiral plunges downward from there.

Bury it!

Do you catch the drift? So you have had some negative team experiences in the past. Join the club. We all have. The difference is that some of us let the dead bury their own dead and move on, while others of us choose to tote the corpse of every bad team experience we have endured.

My advice is that you bury it; don't carry it! Each new team deserves a fresh start—a square chance to prove itself on its own merits. By allowing past sour experiences to override your thinking toward teams, you commit a terrible prejudicial crime against your fellow members—to say nothing of pitting yourself against the Kingdom good that could emerge by working together with others.

Sure, the hurts are real and the wounds are deep. Maybe your experiences truly were atrocious. You have every justification *in the world* to avoid investing in another team after you have been hurt so badly. Yes, you have every reason *in the world* to never join another team again. Every reason *in the world* is yours for the picking. But, my dear wounded friend, you have no reason *in the Kingdom.*

In the Kingdom

In the world, you are justified for holding to the past. In the world, you find superficial company with other wounded souls who team up against working together, and who wallow in the drug of self-pity. But the Kingdom functions differently than the world.

In the Kingdom, you are never justified for holding to the past. In the Kingdom, the call is one of relinquishment and new beginnings. Even as Jesus calls us to forgive seventy times seven (Matt. 18:22), the Spirit compels us to relinquish the past as many times as it takes to live free.

God wants us to embody the essence of the new beginning. When you join a new team, you should be a breath of fresh air. Never be the stench of death. It is about carrying yourself as a "servant of a new covenant" (2 Cor. 3:6), a force of redemption and the total package of God's all-reconciling power.

This is only the first adjustment in the posture of

relinquishment. But it is an important first adjustment. Every member of your team should examine the contents of their garage, and get rid of any past negative experience that casts a shadow on the team.

Think of it: A team whose members have relinquished the past. Just think of it. What power and liberty can flow through such a team. Now, make it so.

Day 7
Relinquishment Adjustment

Flipside

Yesterday's adjustment summoned you to relinquish past negative team experiences, and to give each new team a clean page. It was a call to drop all dead weight, and to approach each new group with innocent expectation that things can be different this time around.

Today we look at the flipside. Positive experiences also need relinquishing. Really great memories about teams you served in yesteryear can do as much damage as the bad ones, if you let them color the new picture. It's a different side of the same coin.

Unfair measure

Let's say you and I have become friends. What if I keep referring to past friends—over and over again? Would you tolerate story upon story of the time I had some great adventure with a previous friend? Maybe initially, but it would get old fast. For our friendship to last, we need to build our own memories.

No one likes to sit through endless stories, or to be judged by the measuring stick of the past. This is true in part because we were not there to experience another person's past, but also because no one can live up to such stories. Good memories often lead to unfair measures.

Potentially great personal friendships die daily from unfair measures. The same goes for teams. To prevent this from happening to your team, I suggest relinquishing all team experiences—bad and good—because all are subject to inaccurate memory.

Inaccurate memory

Our memory of the past is rarely impartial, and is never constant. We tend to make the bad parts of the past *really* bad, and the good parts *really* good. Better, in fact, than they really were. Much of this has to do with what mood we're in.

The act of adding detail or grandeur to a story is called embellishment. It builds up previous good times to mythic proportion. The sentence usually begins with a fond, "I remember when my old team…", and ends with the speaker staring off into space, a glimmer of satisfaction twinkling in the eye.

Not that embellishment is always evil. Without it, a woman would never become pregnant twice. Because of it, after delivering her first child the previous nine months of hormone swings, odd cravings, unwelcome body changes, and sleepless nights somehow lose their sting. They are numbed by the anesthetic of nostalgia. Without embellishment friends would have a difficult time reminiscing about the good old days, the war stories of heroes would be slightly less shiny, and the wonderful world of reminiscence would disappear from the face of the earth.

But embellishment can also be a curse, especially when it comes to teams. A team comprised of members given to embellishment of past team experiences will have a difficult go at their new journey. No team can measure up to myth-sized meanderings down memory lane. If you are convinced that a past team you served on was the be-all and end-all, then we cannot serve together on a new team effectively. Whatever we do will always come up short. The new leader is always lesser than the old; the new members are always lacking in talent and ability comparatively.

Who can compete with fantasy! Tall tales make the future way too small in the shadow of a past made much too big. Any attempt to measure the present by the past success is as inaccurate as passing off a three-inch ruler as a foot. Each measurement is off because your interpretation of the instrument is flawed.

That's nice

Ideally, every member of your team will posture themselves to relinquish the past. In reality, some will do the opposite. How do you handle their stories? A lesson from ancient textual interpretation might help.

There is a rule in ancient textual interpretation that says to always go with the more difficult reading when faced with two texts. Where two texts recount the same story but in different detail and grandeur, the rule of thumb is that the simpler account is probably closer to the original. Whoever authored the more expanded account likely embellished or filled it in.

For example, read the Lord's Prayer in Matthew 6:9-13 and compare it with the Lord's Prayer in Luke 11:2-4. The Lukan version is more stripped down, whereas the Matthean version is more filled out. Without taking away from the doctrine of divine inspiration of scripture, Luke's version is more likely closer to the original. It is more likely that Jesus spoke the version in Luke and that Matthew filled it out (like a preacher who expounds on a text for an audience), than that Jesus spoke the version in Matthew and that Luke stripped it down.

Your lesson is this: When you hear a team member recount a story from another team experience, suspend your judgment on whether it is or is not the full truth. Say, "That's nice," and move on. Other accounts of the same story probably exist plus or minus some details. Maybe the person is telling the truth; maybe some embellishment is involved. In the absence of other accounts, you just cannot be sure. Human nature is to embellish, so understand that they are probably reporting the high points—and making them a little higher.

What matters most is that you do not allow their shadow to eclipse your light. Live in the moment. Take off the rose-colored history glasses. Be present. This is your day. The best is yet to come—and no, it does not have to look like the past others paint! God has newness up his sleeve!

But what if...

Ok, but what if something truly great did happen in the past? What if I am not embellishing when I report history? Here are some suggestions if you have had some great experiences you do not wish to forget.

First, do what Mary did after the birth of Christ and visitation by the shepherds: "But Mary treasured up all these things, pondering them in her heart" (Lk. 2:19). In other words, really allow the experience and memory to impact you at the deepest level. Take home the lessons and store them in your personal diary.

Second, share with others what God did only when appropriate. It may be that what God did is something you should report to future teams you serve on. Or, it may be that God would prefer you keep quiet about it. He has his reasons for secrecy sometimes. Remember, sometimes Jesus forbade people he healed from sharing the news publicly (cf., Lk. 5:14), and other times he even concealed his own identity!

A personal example of how this plays out might help. Several years ago I led a house church that drew some three hundred people in the course of ten months. No embellishment, it is just the truth. Fast forward to today. I am planting a unique ministry that is to be comprised largely of house churches. These are highly autonomous units with well-trained leaders. When first casting the vision for such a church, I used the story of the three hundred people coming through our previous house church to inspire others to join the team and to illustrate to the team what is possible through this type of ministry.

Then it happened. One day I was sharing the story as usual and I felt a classic check in my spirit.

You know what I'm talking about. *It was God.* His message to me was that he was done using the story, at least for now. I was to write it down for people to read, but I was not to refer to it anymore. He very clearly commanded me to share it no more with the teams we were forming.

There could be any number of reasons why he gave that order. Maybe I would become so wrapped up in the memory that I would be no good in the current vision. Maybe the new teams would feel paralyzed at the thought of measuring up to that standard, and some people might quit out of premature discouragement. Or, maybe God himself just grew tired of hearing about what he did in the past, and wanted us to believe for greater things in the future!

The posture of relinquishment is about being on call from God to say what he wants when he wants it...and on the flipside, to be silent when silence is due. The power to break into tomorrow depends on it.

Day 8
Relinquishment Adjustment

Issues of control

On to other areas for relinquishment. In this adjustment, the "C" word is front and center. No not cancer. (Though it might as well be.) The C word I'm speaking of is control. Members of teams everywhere, relinquish your need for control!

A classic

As issues go, control issues are a classic. Like St. Augustine's *City of God* is to spirituality, and like C.S. Lewis' *The Chronicles of Narnia* is to creative writing, control issues are to problems contributing to team disintegration. They are all classics.

Unlike Augustine's and Lewis' works, control issues are not good classics. If there were a master list of issues that mature team members wish would just go away, it would be topped by control issues. Unfortunately, as with all classics—and much like cancer—issues pertaining to control die hard. They simply do not want to go away!

Where and why

Control issues die hard because of where they come from and why they continue to have a place to thrive. As for where they come from, we can sum it up in human nature.

Human nature is to territorialize. Whatever territory we inhabit becomes a place from which to dominate. Have you ever met a receptionist who treated you like scum? That is a function of that person's territorializing of the position. Maybe you did make a mistake that warranted the receptionist's frustration; but at the end of the day the biggest mistake you made was stepping into their territory. You are now in their control.

And why do control issues die hard? Because we who carry them refuse to die! People just like you and me are the hosts for this terrible parasite, not just the receptionist. Control issues live in all of us. They feed off us. As long as they find a willing host in you or me, control issues will continue like leeches with our teams.

So then, should all controlling people keel over and die like Ananias and Sapphira? Of course not! But a dying of some sort is in order. Since we are talking about Christ-followers, might a visit to the cross be the answer? The only way I know of for a controlling person to loosen his or her grip is to spend some time at—or perhaps even on—the cross.

The cross

Let's reflect for a few moments on the cross and its power to deliver us from control issues and help us posture for relinquishment. From a gory physical standpoint, we would rather think of another option, since the cross is the premier instrument of death ever conceived by the mind of man. But from an enlightened spiritual standpoint, the cross is the place of ultimate surrender. The call to the cross is primarily a call away from control and into a life of radical relinquishment. This is a good thing!

Consider the position of a man on a cross. Perhaps even take yourself there now. Arms are outstretched. No possibility to embrace anything. Wrists are pinned and palms are bared wide open. No chance to grip anything. The entire figure is fixed in such as way as to be at the mercy of the elements. Personal control is out the window. You are surrendered.

This is where you and every member of the team need to be. Next time you are together sitting in a circle, posture your spirits in this way. Everyone to your right and left going all the way around the room must hang willingly on their cross, or the meeting should not begin.

If not...

In plain English, this means that the meeting should not begin until every control issue is dealt with. I repeat. Delay the start of the meeting until everyone is on his or her cross. If a single individual resists the cross, the outcome will be impure. Each member will be gripping at this or grasping at that, attempting to control some aspect of the process. Power struggles are likely to result. Much like basketball players from opposite teams wrestling on the court over a loose ball, so will the members of your own team! Before you know it, what should have been a godly meeting has now turned into a free-for-all.

Since dominant ones tend to crowd out those who are more subdued, the former will likely gain the most control. Or at least the appearance of it. So then it will be the overt aggressors against the passive aggressors. This all may take place under the radar, or it may be obvious and in your face, but either way an unholy and counterproductive dynamic will set in.

I implore you, get on the cross today! Each of you on the team, to your crosses you must go. "For the word of the cross is to those who are perishing foolishness, but to us who are being saved it is the power of God" (1 Cor. 1:18).

Day 9
Relinquishment Adjustment

Rabbit trails

There is so much to cover to get our teams postured for power! A book ten times this size could be written. Somehow, I have to decide on a set number of topics, and let the rest go. To attempt to cover everything having to do with teams in a slim book such as this would be foolish. I cannot do it all.

Ah, do you get it? *Neither can your team do it all.* God has formed you for a very specific purpose. You must force yourselves ruthlessly to relinquish all other purposes but that to which God has called you. Everything you do—and I mean everything—must fit a specific God-ordained track.

No deviations. No rabbit trails!

Dissertations and you

You probably know that a dissertation is the final requirement for the Ph.D. degree. Many Ph.D. students work tediously long hours for up to seven years before completing it. Because of this, the average man on the street assumes a dissertation must be a huge document covering virtually every domain in the student's given field. At least that is what I thought.

Actually, the opposite is true. Two years ago I entered a Ph.D. program, and was surprised to discover this fact. In an opening talk on the program requirements, the associate dean explained the dissertation differently. He said, "Consider a forest. Your dissertation is not the forest. Consider the trees. Your dissertation is not the trees. Consider just one tree. Your dissertation is not even one tree. Consider a single branch and twig on that one tree. Wrong again, your dissertation is not those. Consider a caterpillar on the twig. You guessed it; your dissertation is not even the caterpillar. Do you want to know what your dissertation is? It's a single hair on the caterpillar's back."

What does this have to do with you and your team? Simply this: Your purpose for existing is not the forest, or the trees, or a single tree, or a branch or twig on a single tree. It is not the caterpillar. Your purpose is a single hair on the back of the caterpillar that is slinking along on the twig…connected to the branch…growing from the tree…alongside the other trees…forming a forest. Unless you narrow it down that finely, get used to the rabbit trails because you will be spending more time on those than on the path of purpose.

Precision excellence

Maybe another illustration will help. You probably know the concept of a shotgun. Rather than firing a single bullet, shotgun cartridges are packed with tiny ball-like ammunition that fan out after the trigger is pulled.

While the shotgun serves many purposes, there are some purposes for which it is not useful. One of them is sharp shooting. A sharpshooter, be he a sniper in the enemy bush or an Olympic sportsman, would never use a shotgun. When precision purpose is called for, better weapons than shotguns exist.

Make the connection to your team. The shotgun approach is not the one to take. Sharp shooting is the way to go. A shotgun team may claim great effectiveness because they are doing "so much," but the precision team is truly effective.

Members of precision teams have narrowed down specifically what God has called them to do, and they have developed a tremendous amount of skill in doing it. God is more apt to share his power with them because he knows it will not go to waste firing at anything that moves. People are more apt to call on the team when a need arises because it has earned the rank of specialist.

This is a matter of excellence—relinquishing the desire to cover the whole forest or to fire too broad of blasts. It is about avoiding the extraneous to focus on the excellent. Even as it is a proven fact that companies known for a particular brand are better off sticking with that brand than diversifying, so it is with teams. Find your target, your market, your mission, and set your sights sharply on it. Locate that one hair on the caterpillar's back, and become expert in picking it off. This is where excellence is born!

God desires excellence in his Kingdom teams. Become a mouthpiece of excellence, not a blow horn of haphazardness. Consider what Peter has to say about this subject: "But you are a chosen race...that you may proclaim the excellencies of

Him who has called you out of the darkness into His marvelous light; Beloved, I urge you as aliens and strangers to abstain from fleshly lusts, which wage war against the soul. Keep your behavior excellent among the Gentiles" (1 Pet. 2:9,11,12).

Excellencc is a byproduct of precision. Precision is a byproduct of relinquishment. Shut yourselves away and do not leave until you have relinquished all of the rabbit trails, and until you have gotten precise with your mission. This may take hours; but you have no choice. After that, begin working to develop excellence at "this one thing." Watch how God comes through. He will be so pleased!

Team lust

The Holy Spirit desires that you fight off the lust to bite off more than you can chew, in order to accomplish his clear-cut objective for bringing you together. Yes, a team needs to fight off lust just like individuals.

Do not deceive yourselves. Even as individuals have lusts for doing the wrong things, so do teams. If you continually feel your team pulled in several directions, then that is temptation, and it is normal. If your team continually chases after all those directions, then that is lust, and it needs to be overcome.

This is a word for all Kingdom teams. Locate the mark God has called you to take out. Relinquish the remainder. God has other teams in place too, you know. Your team is not called to do it all, or even to do most of it.

Lust is never satisfied. It does not speak the

language of contentment. God cannot share his power with teams who cannot learn contentment. They become like a massive black hole, swallowing everything yet giving up nothing.

Get back to the basics, and lose the need to be all things. God empowers teams who know what they are about and stick to it.

Day 10
Relinquishment Adjustment

Log jammed!

Let's take relinquishment to another level today. The concepts in this adjustment are rich, but you may have to really think them through on your own and as a team to achieve maximum impact. I will lay out the concept as best I can, but your participation is needed. Up for discussion is how to deal with logjams.

What teams do

Teams exist because problems exist. The effective team comes up with workable solutions to address the problems. It also thinks ahead some steps to avoid potential problems. So, at the end of the day, every team does essentially the same thing: Work with ideas.

Boiled down, all teams are idea-driven. Teams with the best and freshest ideas come out on top. Sports teams work with ideas in the form of complex plays that win. Business teams work with ideas in the form of plans, campaigns, and strategies. Ministry teams work with ideas in similar form. Ideas, ideas, ideas.

Since teams work with ideas, creativity is needed. Anyone can have a bright idea now and then, but creativity in combining them is another story. The question—and the subject of this adjustment—is this: What happens when the ideas and creativity become jammed? What should you do when the team gets stumped? Read on.

Idea block

If you are a writer, you are familiar with something called "writer's block." You know you have it when the screen has been blank for fifteen minutes, and when your mind registers even blanker. Surely the ideas are there, but either they are so cluttered that you cannot sort them out, or your brain just seems to be out to lunch.

Teams experience idea blocks, or logjams, as well. Even the most precision-oriented cooperative team finds itself periodically at an impasse concerning what to do next and how to do it.

It is not uncommon. Your team is gathered in a strategic planning meeting. At issue is how specifically to execute a certain plan that fits into the precise mission you have already agreed upon. The trouble is that the dry erase board is blank. Yawns are beginning to surface. Frustration is knocking at the door, and it wants in the room. Stagnancy hangs heavily in the air. Though your overall mission is precise, on this particular day the well of ideas is dry as a bone.

Or maybe the logjam is of a different sort. The whole team is gathered eagerly around the dry erase board. Flow charts and bullet points and brainstorms clutter the board in many shades of pretty colors—the fruit of brilliant team thinking. Additional notes are strewn out upon the board table. Creativity has been in the air. Now before you stand five distinct options, each of which could work well in theory. The trouble is that each idea is so good that the team does not know which to choose.

Both of these situations can be classified as logjams. Simply put, the team has hit a wall.

Options

After hitting a wall, you have options. One option is to put on another pot of double-caffeinated coffee and push through. You can order in, work late, and burn the midnight oil until you hammer out a solution. This is the hard way. And the results are rarely excellent. Quality suffers.

Or, you can take a second option—which just so happens to be much smarter and easier. You can acknowledge that a logjam exists, and exercise the posture of relinquishment right then and there. You do this by suspending the meeting until the time is right to take it up again. You can pray, walk away, and come back to it later when you are fresh. You can intelligently exercise the posture of relinquishment by temporarily surrendering to the logjam until an opportune time.

But, isn't walking away the same as quitting? Would it not be a sign of weakness to leave before reaching the solution? Why not dig in deeper and push through and get it done now? Are we "spiritual" or not?

Because haste makes…

Friend, pushing is not always spiritual. Sometimes the path of least resistance is the one to take. Relinquishment rightly timed is your friend, and it is a sign of maturity.

Take a lesson from the Creation Narrative (Gen. 1-2). Do you see God frantically working to put a bow on creation in a single day? Of course not! He wisely took his time; and he even built in a period for relaxation.

Did God get log jammed? Of course not. But God did set forth a principle of relinquishment that we can learn from. He worked some, and then he paused. It was a cycle he repeated until the project of creation was done. Work. Pause.

Methodological, unforced, leisurely creativity is preferred to the rush. Like the confusion caused by a run-on sentence, an unpunctuated meeting serves no purpose but to debilitate creative minds. It is better to call a break without resolution than to push through and emerge with an inherently flawed solution because you were too proud to retreat and regroup. What a grand nugget of wisdom!

The posture of relinquishment has many applications, but this is one of the most important. You must learn to let go. In a flash, the logjam will dissolve and the creative ideas will flow freely once again.

More on this tomorrow.

Day 11
Relinquishment Adjustment

Breakthrough

If yesterday's adjustment left you wondering, "Ok…now what?," then good. Be not troubled, you are becoming positioned to breakthrough all logjams. "'Not by might, nor by power, but by My Spirit,' says the LORD of hosts" (Zech. 4:6).

Learn to relinquish; watch the power of God move mountains.

Translation

Let me illustrate how relinquishment works on a personal level to produce breakthrough. This may help bridge the gap to how it works in teams. Years ago, my Greek professor gave us this advice. "When working on a translation, you will run into the occasional mental block. There you will find yourself, staring blankly at a sentence whose vocabulary you know and whose grammar you understand; and yet the translation simply will not come. At that moment," he advised, "get up and walk away. Go for a walk, grab something to eat, but whatever you do, release your thoughts from the sentence. If you will follow this simple advice, when you return to the table the translation usually will jump out at you suddenly!"

And it did. Time and again when working through the Greek texts, my mind would suddenly freeze. At first, being immature and not wanting to give up, I would attempt to push through. I would ignore the instructor's advice. With time, I realized he was right and I was wrong. I quickly learned to spot the onset of an impassible mental block—of the logjam we dealt with yesterday—and without wasting even a moment I would jump up and walk away. When later I returned, the vast majority of the time the sentence would indeed come alive virtually immediately.

Breakthrough!

This sort of advice also applies in many areas of team life, not just to an individual working in an archaic language. It is why a football team can go into halftime stomped, but return to dominate the rest of the game. Similarly, it is why your team may be at an impasse concerning its next strategic move; but after exercising intelligent relinquishment come back together and see the right path clear as day. It is nothing short of a phenomenon; and it is nothing less than real.

Choked out

What explains this principle? A teaching of Jesus in the parable of the seed and soils holds the answer. The seed represents the gospel—or any Kingdom idea. The soils represent the recipients of the idea. As the parable goes, Jesus laments that some "have heard the word, and the worries of the world, and the deceitfulness of riches and the desires for other things enter in and choke the word, and it becomes unfruitful" (Mk. 4:18-19).

Brilliant! Isn't this how it goes so often? The reason so many breakthroughs are held at bay is that we become entangled, frustrated, confused as though caught in a web. Or, to continue the theme, as though trapped in a logjam. But if we will just learn the value of relinquishment—the strategic and timely stepping back from entanglements—then the idea will be free to grow and bear fruit!

Be assured, a right path exists just beyond the barrier your team is now facing. Breakthrough is not just some modern-day flimsy catch phrase. Since your team is an agent of God, it is his desire that every idea he plants in you bears fruit. When that happens, the Kingdom is expanded—meaning God receives the glory and man receives the blessing. What could be better?

Search yourselves

What sorts of breakthrough-blocking concerns is your team holding? What is choking the good seed of its life? Are you over-taxed, over-spent, and over-worked? Is your team willing to pause, breathe deeply, and re-posture itself when necessary in order to achieve breakthrough, even if it looks like the opposite might occur by backing down temporarily?

Does a corporate fear of failure control you? Perhaps a defeatist attitude has overtaken the group? Or could it be a naïve standard of perfection that is holding you back—in other words, are you aiming at impossible standards or deadlines?

Listen carefully. Time is on your side…if only

you learn to work time to your advantage. It is all about time. If you are always behind the eight ball, always in a reactionary stance rather than a relaxed anticipatory posture, then time is your worst enemy and your fiercest conqueror. If every decision you make has to be made *right now*, may I suggest you are moving at the *wrong speed*?

Take it down a notch. Unwind those gears. Adjust the idle of your team to a more even hum. Pressure is the enemy of sound strategic decisions. Sure, pressure produces diamonds; but that is pressure of a different kind. It is a slow, steady pressure, not the breakneck, stressful type. Remember, diamonds are never produced in an all-nighter!

Even as I write, my team and I have several ideas that we have been working out for months and years. Wherever possible, I like to give ideas plenty of time to percolate through a series of meetings and breaks. The work-pause or struggle-relinquish cycle has never failed to produce great outcomes. Powerful execution nearly always follows.

Has your team recently found itself log jammed? Then find solace in this psalm: "Teach me Thy way, O LORD, and lead me in a *level path*, because of my foes. I would have despaired unless I had believed that I would see the goodness of the LORD in the land of the living. *Wait* for the LORD; Be strong, and let your heart take courage; Yes, *wait* for the LORD" (Ps. 27: 11,13-14, italics added).

Relinquish. Wait. His breakthrough power of illumination and enlightenment will come.

III

Posture of Separation

Be of sober spirit, be on the alert.
1 Peter 5:8a

Day 12
Separation Adjustment

Actions of one

The posture of separation has many varied applications to teams. Before moving into some of the more colorful applications, we are going to deal with the most obvious: Positioning for purity.

God does not have to explain why we must be pure, or why he punishes impurity. He is bound neither to our courts nor to our whims. God is not some arbitrary punisher that delights in catching us doing evil; yet he is no chump either. He sets laws into effect, and he enforces them. Yes, Kingdom law applies even in this New Covenant era. Sin is sin. Transgressions have consequences.

Enter the posture of separation. It is a serious posture, whose neglect none can afford. Being linked to a Kingdom team only raises the stakes.

Fine print

Do you not know? Have you not heard? Your willful sins have consequences—and not just for you. They hurt the whole team!

Miriam's sin of murmuring put the entire people of Israel in a holding pattern for seven days. "So Miriam was shut up outside the camp for seven days, and the people did not move on until Miriam was received again" (Num. 12:5)

Achan's sin of coveting items from Jericho that God had placed under the ban led to Israel's sore defeat at the hands of Ai. "But the sons of Israel acted unfaithfully in regard to the things under the ban, for Achan...took some of the things under the ban, therefore the anger of the LORD burned against the sons of Israel" (Josh. 7:1).

Before you shrug this off as Old Covenant only, look at the immorality in the Corinthian church. "It is actually reported that there is immorality among you...and you have become arrogant and have not mourned... Your boasting is not good. Do you not know that a little leaven leavens the whole lump of dough?" (1 Cor. 5:1-2, 6).

This is the fine print in God's rules for blessing or not blessing a team. Seven of your eight members may be living righteously; but if one is carrying on, then the entire will suffer. Yes, God does hold you each individually accountable for your lives (Ezek. 18:1-4); but by virtue of being joined in a team he also holds you corporately accountable. In the same way that sin entered through Adam and affected the entire race, so does sin work through a team.

Could this be why?

If your team has been lacking in the power of God to accomplish its Kingdom tasks, and if you have searched high and low for the cause but cannot locate it, maybe the cause is sin in the camp.

Sometimes we perform diagnoses of the organization and neglect the diagnosis of the heart. You know the deal: "for God sees not as man sees, for man looks at the outward appearance, but the LORD looks at the heart" (1 Sam. 16:7). A single misaligned heart within your team is more than a little problem. For if God's power on the team requires his favorable gaze, and if the gaze of God becomes unfavorable, then only two outcomes are possible. One outcome is that God brings calamity upon the team as he did to Israel so many times. The other option is that God simply withdraws his favor and allows you to go it alone.

Neither option is happy! Depending on the Kingdom weight your team bears, the ramifications could affect even more than just your team. Therefore, may I suggest a course of action? My suggestion is simple enough for a child to understand. *Clean your house.*

Clean house!

A good place to begin is with a time of deep searching on the part of every member. Perhaps a month of consecration-style prayer and fasting is in order. Hey, if God's power and glory have departed, then deep searching ought to be the singular priority. Whether your team is explicitly for "church" or not if it is a Kingdom team then it must follow Kingdom principles. Prayer and fasting is a Kingdom principle; and it is the first step in the process and posture of separation.

Another part of the initial posturing process might be some good old-fashioned confession between members. Confession is like a beaming spotlight. When the light is on, the rats are gone. James pleads, "Therefore, confess your sins to one another, and pray for one another, so that you may be healed" (Jms. 5:16). He goes on to write a line that showcases the redemptive power of team: "My brethren, if any among you strays from the truth, and one turns him back, let him know that he who turns a sinner from the error of his way will save his soul from death, and will cover a multitude of sins" (5:19-20). Hallelujah!

But we also need to prepare ourselves for a not so sweet ending. As with any good cleaning, sometimes this requires removal of and parting with things near and dear. In the case of your team, it may even entail removing or parting with a member or two who refuses to change. The thought of this to any warm-hearted believer is positively chilling; but the alternative is that you become an accessory. Harboring a willful rebel is like being one yourself. Personally, if I have to choose a side, I'll go with God.

Ongoing

The true posture of separation is, of course, ongoing and touches every aspect of our lives. When we are postured for separation, every gate—eyes, ears, taste, touch, smell, and whatever sixth senses you want to throw in there—is guarded against unholy invasion. A state of consecration permeates our being, such that we stand at attention before the Throne for Kingdom worship and service at all times. The posture of separation is, in a very real way, the ready position of the believer. And it is the ready position of the team.

Now the question comes to you: Is the posture of separation the current position of your team? Can you honestly say that as a group you are separate from willful sin?

Are *you* pure? Honestly?

Day 13
Separation Adjustment

S - -

We believers often refer to the "fire of God." This metaphor illustrates his power—the aspect that purifies. We also use fire to describe something that is the absolute opposite of purity: Lust and sexual impurity. This type of fire consumes everyone in its path.

Teams that are postured for separation create distance from the lust fire so God will send his fire. Get this adjustment wrong and the fire will fall. Not the good kind of fire, but the bad—the fire of lust that respects nobody and no body.

Today we tackle sexual separation.

An easy pitfall

Misguided and inappropriate sexual activity between members of Kingdom teams presents an easy—almost ready-made pitfall. Ready-made because we are sexual creatures. Like eating, drinking, sleeping, and other instinctual functions, sex comes naturally to most everyone. Unfortunately for many Kingdom teams, this rule plays out all too freely as lust burns through the ranks.

This point is proved daily. Single people hooking up sexually, married persons forsaking spouses, coarse jesting and innuendo running rampant—these things and more can be found in Kingdom teams across the land.

Unbounded sexuality creates a huge power drain in our teams. Every volt of power God sends becomes twisted and turned on ourselves for carnal pleasure. The time, energy, and resources with which God has blessed us to help others, are squandered in a vain search for that one experience that will once and for all satisfy.

But the sex drive is never satisfied—and lust let loose in a team *will* consume the whole lot! "There are three things that will not be satisfied. Four that will not say, "Enough!" (Pr. 30:15). The fire of lust is one of those things. It is hungry enough to devour the whole team, and the team must posture itself against it. The way to do this is through proper separation.

Sexual separation

Please do not believe your team to be beyond sexual sin. Precautions are a sound idea for every team, regardless of age, purpose, gender make up, and time spent together. Corporately and individually, the team must determine to enact measures and guards to keep improper sexuality out.

Let's begin with the obvious. Coarse jesting is never appropriate. "…And there must be no filthiness and silly talk, or coarse jesting, which are not fitting…" (Eph. 5:4).

Also inappropriate is flirting, particularly if you are married. How do you tell if you are flirting? If your tone of voice changes when speaking with the opposite sex, then you are flirting. I tell married men that if they would not speak to me in a certain tone of voice, then they should not use that tone when speaking with women. This goes not only for speaking with female team members, but for speaking with females anywhere—in the grocery line, gas pump, on the job…anywhere.

If you are a female, this holds for you as well. Do not speak to a man in a tone different than you would speak to another woman. Keep your hands to yourself except for a holy hug, lasso those batting eyes, and maintain a presentable appearance and posture. That's a nice way of saying to keep "it" from being "out" and on display.

Single folk, just be led by the Holy Spirit. (Keyword: *Holy* Spirit.) Your future mate might be on your team. An approach might be necessary. Mutual attractions may develop, leading to marriage. Only keep it pure. Keep it pure.

Expect the unexpected

Those instructions are obvious. We do not always follow them, but they are obvious nonetheless. Even if you are guarded on those fronts, you still need to expect the unexpected and guard for blind spots.

One blind spot is that person of the opposite sex to whom you are not necessarily attracted. You may feel strong with this person. Strong enough to work late alone, to take a business road trip together, to have extended telephone conversations regarding personal matters. But watch out! Lust knows no boundaries. It will spark a fire with just a shred of tinder. You may wind up in bed with the very person you thought was unattractive only a month ago.

This is just one example. It is up to you and your team to guard against the unexpected so you are not caught off guard yourself. Remember, the devil prowls. The definition of prowl is to roam stealthily. Anything he can do to separate you from the fire of God and baptize you in the fire of lust is fair game.

Leads to power

If you apply these separation adjustments rightly, expect the power of God to come upon your team mightily. Peter said we are "a holy nation" (1 Pet. 2:9), a people possessed by God and not by fleshly trappings. Upon that holy nation the fire of God falls (Acts 2).

He is standing by, just waiting for your team to separate itself in the right ways and for the right reasons. I would remind you gently but firmly: The desire of God is that your team would be a channel of his unadulterated power. For this to happen, you too must be unadulterated. Yes, I understand grace just fine and I hope you do too. Separation is not a matter of thinking we can work for salvation. It is about making ourselves available, usable, and poised as pure channels.

Do you like the sound of that? Do you want to be a pure channel? Separation is worth it.

Day 14
Separation Adjustment

Unified not suffocated

Over the next four days, we are going to discuss in-depth another aspect of the posture of separation: The establishment and maintenance of proper borders and boundaries between team members. Assuming you understand that the posture of separation first and foremost relates to purity, we can address other aspects now.

You may be surprised to know that the posture of separation involves more than merely abstaining from the world and living rightly. It also has application to how we relate to one another, and to how we create space between one another to avoid togetherness becoming torturous. Holiness is indisputably important; but so is keeping the right distance between each other.

Unity

How do we relate to one another? Or maybe I should ask, how are we *supposed* to relate to one another? Scripture teaches that we are to be "diligent to preserve the unity of the Spirit in the bond of peace" (Eph. 4:3). Luke reports that the earliest believers "were together, and had all things in common" (Acts 2:44). It is in this unity that God's power is made known through us to the world (see Jn. 17:23).

Those are great ideals, but my question is: What does unity mean in practical terms? How should my team apply the principle of unity? What does it look like to be united of the Spirit and to have all things in common?

Does it mean I must trade all of my individuality? That I cease any and all private ownership? That I forfeit personal space, and keep an open door to anyone, anytime, anywhere? That I let down all of my boundaries and borders, and say, "Come one, come all. I'm open for business all of the time!"

For goodness sakes, I hope not! A more sensible and sane definition of biblical unity must exist. But what is it?

A definition

May I suggest a definition of unity? Be warned, it is a bit crude and probably will not win a Pulitzer; but this definition should do the trick. *Biblical unity exists where two or more likeminded believers (in our case team members) walk with intimate togetherness in a common path, without turning the intimate togetherness into tortured suffocation.*

Unity may be biblical, but it is also a buzzword loaded with misunderstandings—like a hot potato with way too much on top. A little known secret to team unity is team separation. Too much separation, and you have division. Too little separation, and you have suffocation—tortured suffocation. At last check, that is not a good thing!

Illustration from marriage

My wife and I challenge couples to do something unconventional before walking down the aisle, and to pay it extra effort during the first year. We tell them that it is a key to unity and to the health of the marriage. We explain that it may seem abnormal and cold, but in actual fact it is the key to a relationship that is built to last. What is this unconventional counsel? Establish borders and boundaries with one another.

A seasoned pastor once said, "We need to learn to come in and out of each other's worlds without leaving a trail of chaos." And he was speaking on the topic of marriage!

A marriage that lasts is one in which the spouses have an amazing chemistry and oneness, while at the same time a deep respect that allows husband and wife space to grow as individuals. For example, my wife Katie and I have known one another for seventeen years as of this writing. In so many ways, we are one. We are best of friends. Quite often we will blurt out the same exact words in a particular situation; or after one says something the other will respond, saying, "I was just about to say the same exact thing!" The time we spend together is always fun. Truly, we have a partnership to be envied.

At the same time, over the course of the years we have discovered unique rhythms and patterns in each of us. We are walking an identical path in intimate togetherness, yet our mindfulness of each other's individuality enables us to do so without stepping on the other's toes. And, without suffocating each other to death.

Borders and boundaries

Borders and boundaries, mapped in just the right measure, enable us to enjoy uncommon unity. It seems the reverse of conventional wisdom. Yet it is true. Because we deeply respect each other as individuals, and because we give one another the necessary space to be who we are, the uncommon unity we share is possible.

Can borders and boundaries help your team? You bet! They can help you to keep from being burned out on one another. They can help you to maintain appropriate and pure relationships between the sexes. They can help you to cultivate a sense of longing to be together, and a desire to take advantage of every moment you have together. They can prevent misunderstandings and intrusions that are passable every once in a while, but are positively poisonous in frequency. Borders and boundaries can do all this and more.

For today's adjustment, take stock of the borders and boundaries in your team (or the lack thereof). Ponder the following questions. Really take your time with them.

- What are some borders and boundaries I would really like from my team members?
- What borders and boundaries are being routinely crossed, leaving me feeling suffocated?

- Which people are crossing these borders and boundaries?
- What are some borders and boundaries individual members need from me?
- Putting myself in the shoes of fellow team members, can I think of anyone whose borders and boundaries I might have crossed in the past?
- Am I willing to respect the borders and boundaries of fellow team members, even if I do not understand them fully?

Be reminded, how you respond to these questions has bearing on the amount of power God can place on your team. He cannot empower a team that fails to honor one another's space, because that team won't be around long enough to steward it. The team will disintegrate under its own weight.

Day 15
Separation Adjustment

Sensitivity

Many teams have at least one. And it is one too many. It's the insensitive member—the one who seems clueless to the borders and boundaries of everyone, and who honors the borders and boundaries of no one.

Such a person hinders the power of God by disrupting the equilibrium of the team members. Whether intentionally or not, their thoughtless actions invite spite that even the purest of saints struggles to resist. Worse than that, it invites a curse. Deuteronomic law reads, "You shall not move you neighbor's boundary mark. Cursed is he who moves his neighbor's boundary mark" (Deut. 19:14, 27:17).

This posture adjustment is dedicated as a plea to the insensitive that the curse might be avoided. Watch how you treat the boundaries of others!

Example of sensitivity

The tried and true axiom goes something like this: An ounce of prevention is worth a pound of cure. This is certainly true with borders and boundaries. Sensitivity is a great prevention. A personal illustration might clarify.

Recently our team took on an executive leader.

He works closely with me on the operational end of our ministry, so I can be free to focus on providing overall vision and offering spiritual guidance within the organization. For now, financial constraints prohibit hiring him full time, so he works a full time job at a local university. His paid job is quite demanding, so the mere fact that he is even willing to do half of what he is charged to do as executive leader is a testament to his character.

The other morning I awoke with some important footnote thoughts about some strategic planning items we had been going over the previous day. In typical form, I sat down to wrap them into an email, which he could then review as his schedule would permit. This is how we normally conduct business together between our twice-weekly face-to-face meetings.

With my fingers poised on the keyboard, suddenly I felt a strong need to speak with him. Email would not suffice this time. So, shortly after nine o'clock in the morning—when he is normally engaged in his full time job—I placed a call to his cell phone. I interrupted him. We conversed for over an hour, and accomplished a great deal more than we could have over email.

So that means I can dial him up all of the time, right? Wrong! In fact, toward the end of our conversation—without him bringing up the topic—I explained emphatically that such interruptions at work would not be my normal practice. I made it clear that I respect his commitment to take that time out of his busy day to discuss the ministry, but I also respect his need to be intrusion-free as much as possible while at work so as to remain focused on the university. I made it known that calling him like this would not become a regular deal.

Do you see what I was doing? I was establishing some borders and boundaries. I was building in some lines of separation. Not for me, but for him. For him to remain a functioning member of the team, he needs for me to respect some lines *without having to ask that those lines be respected.*

Don't wait until

Please, do not wait until the other person throws up the fences to respect their boundaries. For teams to function in unity, a sense of space should be established. For us, part of the borders and boundaries include me not interrupting his day every time I have a brainstorm about the ministry.

Other practical borders and boundaries needing sensitivity are things like family time, days off, pop-in visits, leaving at the appropriate time when invited over for a meal, and the like. Some people are night owls. Others rise on the wings of the dawn. Families with young children might require a little extra space. One pastor I know has a no-calls rule after nine-thirty p.m. except in absolute emergencies. Everyone is different. Honor their lifestyle.

Success in this adjustment boils down to simple manners. Be polite. Have consideration. Do not charge into a person's world like a bull. When calling a team member, ask whether it is a good time to be calling. Do not follow "hello" with a monologue before making sure you are not interrupting something important.

Everyone's responsibility

Borders and boundaries are everyone's responsibility. You should respect others, and they should respect you. As you witness the habits, dispositions, and preferences of fellow team members, adjust your interactions with them accordingly. I have one team member with whom I check in on a regular basis at six-fifteen in the morning. While that is not a good time for most people, it just happens to be the time that this leader is clocking out of the night shift at work. But were I to apply that calling time to most members, it would be inappropriate. I have a responsibility to know the rhythms of my team members, and to act accordingly.

The responsibility goes both ways. If fellow team members are encroaching on space I need, then I have a duty to let them know. If I fail to speak up, then I am as guilty as they for disturbing the peace.

The point for you

Here is where it comes to a head for you. I have shared very personally how I posture myself for godly separation as a matter of sensitivity toward my team. What are you going to do with your team?

If you are beginning to feel encroached upon by another team member, do not hesitate to lay down some ground rules. It might not be a bad idea to hold an open and honest team discussion on the topic. Allow everyone to vent, to explain their rhythms, and to request sensitivity in certain areas. You do the same.

Paying this adjustment healthy attention will lead to greater mutual respect than less. You can never go wrong with sensitivity. The power of God works mightily through a sensitive team. "Grace be with you" (Col. 4:18).

Day 16
Separation Adjustment

Sharing

The words fly like an arrow from the mouths of concerned parents on the playground. "Sam, Anna! Share!!!" Of all the childhood lessons we should hold dearly throughout our lives, the lesson to "share" ought to be on top of the heap.

But wait. Sharing involves crossing over and becoming part of the world of others. It means ripping up wrongly placed fence posts—those borders and boundaries that we erected out of selfishness rather than purity.

Gotcha! You thought yesterday's separation adjustment gave you permission to sequester yourself, didn't you! Ready or not, some of your fences are about to come down.

Remember when

Remember when mom or grandma hollered from the stuffy hot kitchen, the scent of baked goods filling the air, "Run across the street and borrow a stick of butter!" How about that summer the aging gentleman two doors down needed to borrow the trimmer because his broke, so you gave him free access to your garage? Or recall the days when... You get the point.

Sharing. I'm not saying it is a thing of the past. Well, actually, maybe I am. In these postmodern days as cities are growing taller and city dwellers are growing apart, sharing seems more an unreachable ideal than a practical lifestyle.

It is not the place of this book to lament over the so-called collapse of small town values. Leave that to the porch-sitters who fill Friday nights with winding walks down memory lane. The point of my bringing up how things used to be is to set up for a simple question: What if your team was to share? Community would result.

Common unity

Common. Unity. Sharing produces both. Fuse them together and what does it spell? *Community.*

Community is the hallmark of a powerful team. Outside of community, a team is scattered, weakened, and more susceptible to break ups. Within community, a team is united and able to endure. This is because in community, everyone is reading from the same sheet of music. Togetherness leading to harmony is the result.

How do we reach community? For community to take root two attributes must be in place. First, there must be unity of the right kind. A unity that binds together the team members, with sensitivity to borders and boundaries, ought to be the aim. But unity alone is not enough. The second half of the equation must be in place. The team must have things in *common.*

Let us rest our minds for a few moments on this

word, "common." Speak it aloud so you can feel it. (Whisper if you are around people and do not want to look odd. But it is important for this adjustment that you speak the word so you can hear it.) Common.

There are some words that seem to sound like what they mean. "Juicy" sounds like what it means. "Slimy" sounds like what it means. "Haggard" sounds like what it means. So does common.

Something about that word conjures the sudden crossing of borders and boundaries that have been erected from selfishness more than needfulness. It is a striking word, and not unlike one of those gigantic monster bull dozers like you would see in a world records book. Only this dozer is used to plow walls that would keep us from doing that one thing our parents told us to do but that we never quite got down: share.

Call to share within

The Spirit of God would summon your team to learn to share amongst yourselves. In tangible ways, your team needs to learn to share.

Does someone have a need among you? Share to meet that need. One member of our team needed a car. So my wife and I gave him our car. It was not a car we had up on blocks on the backyard. We drove it daily, and would have continued to drive for many more years had we not signed over the title to him. This is just one example of multiplied dozens. (If I am boasting now, let it be in Christ!) If it were not true I would not say it. We are examples worthy of imitation in the area of sharing sacrificially with team members in need.

And we, too, have received from sharing team members. During a difficult financial time a couple blessed my family with a grocery gift card four months in a row. More immediate on my mind is something occurring as I write this book and recover from my recent back surgery. Without asking them to do it, several members of various teams have stepped in with meals for my family to ease the burden.

This is a word of balance to yesterday's word on borders and boundaries. Your team needs healthy separation to avoid suffocation, but you must not take your borders and boundaries to the extreme such that you neglect common unity. Some members, perhaps even you, have put up some fences that effectively make biblical sharing impossible. You are consumed with filling your own needs; and you thought yesterday's adjustment was another proof that you are right. Well, you are wrong. At the point where our borders and boundaries interfere with sharing in the team, we have gone too far.

From another angle, sharing amongst team members is a critical element in setting you *apart* as a Kingdom team from the teams of the world. And, even better, it sets you up to be a Kingdom team to touch the world!

Call to share outside

Brace yourself, because this is exciting! Once your team has become prolific in sharing with one another, a new dimension of God's power will come upon you to take that spirit of sharing outside to the world.

"But," you argue, "my team is for business, or sports, or school. We are not a church team. How does taking the spirit of sharing to the world apply to us?" No matter! If you are a Kingdom team, you have a call to be salt and light just the same (see Matt. 5:13). The dichotomy between sacred and secular is false. Believers everywhere, on all kinds of teams, are needed to share what they have with the world.

Day 17
Separation Adjustment

Rules for sharing

The topics of these separation adjustments are only as penetrating as our willingness to internalize them. While they seem basic in print—like instructions for putting together that tricycle for your nephew—life has a way of complicating them in dizzying ways.

Finding the right degree of separation and togetherness introduces one such complication. Intimate togetherness is important, but not so much that we suffocate and torture each other. Borders and boundaries are necessary, but not so much that we neglect community and sharing. Likewise, sharing is critical, but not to the degree that we are damaged for giving too much.

Balance is the word of the day. Some rules for sharing might nudge the scales toward the happy medium so we can avoid unnecessary strain.

Recipe for strain

Searching for a recipe for strain in your team relationships? Here's the perfect one: Share your stuff without thinking through the possible consequences—without any rules. Too many friendships have been soured after a seemingly good plan to share an item went south. You may have experienced this firsthand. I have.

Now, we have not excuse to horde our stuff because of a few bad experiences. Jesus would have us to share. He teaches, "Give to him who asks of you, and do not turn away from him who wants to borrow from you" (Matt. 5:42). The key is to recognize the potential strain sharing might place on a relationship, and head off that strain with common-sense biblical rules.

Rules

Rules have not received a fair shake of late. For some reason people see them as evil. I ask you, is the line that separates on-coming highway traffic evil? Is that not a rule? Yes, it is a rule, and a good one at that. It enables drivers to share the road without colliding except in the rare case someone crosses the line unwittingly. So it is with rules for sharing.

There are rules for the borrowers. First, do not borrow what you cannot pay back quickly. "A man lacking in sense pledges, and becomes surety in the presence of his neighbor" (Pr. 17:18). "The borrower becomes the lender's slave" (Pr. 22:7). And certainly, do not borrow what you cannot pay back at all! Being delinquent with a friend amounts to taking advantage of that relationship. No relationship can withstand too many defaults before crumbling.

Second, return what you borrow *in good shape*. If it was working when you borrowed it, return it working. If it was clean, return it clean. If it was not, clean it any way. Treat it better than you "have to." This will preserve your name and make it good. "A good name is to be more desired than great riches, favor is better than silver and gold (Pr. 22:1).

If you are the lender, you have some rules too. First, lend nothing you are unwilling to part with for good. Not all borrowers follow the rules. You may lend an item in good faith and receive it back in bad repair. Too bad. You chose to lend, so you must bear the cost if one is incurred. While the damage may be the other party's fault, you should have prepared yourself for it.

Second, avoid charging interest on money unless you are in the actual business of supplying financial capital. If you are in the money business, make sure the interest you fix is fair. "He who profits illicitly troubles his own house" (Pr. 15:27). Making a profit off a friend or team member is as illicit as can be. If you cannot be generous, be not a lender.

Each of these rules highlights not just a posture of separation, but a posture of relinquishment. Good borrowers relinquish the right to default; good lenders relinquish the right to complain when a default happens. The postures work together.

How to prevent defaults

As good as sharing is, we should conclude this adjustment with an even better way to deal with team members in need. This way prevents defaults, and the whole slew of troubles that surrounds sharing. What it the better way? The better way is to give away.

When seeing someone on your team in need, you have two options. You can outright give to the person, or you can lend. Lending is what we have been discussing. It is the type of sharing where you literally share a particular item with someone else for a period of time. That is to say, they borrow it from you. One summer we shared our lawnmower with a neighbor in this way. We granted access, but we retained ownership.

The other option is to outright give to the person. We gave away our car. The neighbor gives away a stick of butter. That couple gave away those grocery cards to us. Giving away implies a total release of ownership. For good. Returns neither necessary nor expected. Interest is not charged to your account. What was *mine* is now *yours*. I do not want it back.

Truthfully, in most cases outright giving is preferred to lending. When you give to me or vice versa, the thing that is given cannot now come between us. If we choose the lend-borrow option, the potential for strain and strife really opens up because misunderstanding can easily creep in.

If you do choose to lend-borrow within your team, at least follow the rules. And, whether you lend or give, remember that the posture of relinquishment plays a role throughout. Without that posture, sharing of any type is unlikely.

Do it

A team that shares is a team that cares. Your team cannot afford stinginess in its ranks. Go ahead, give something away today. Watch what great effects it has on your team. And watch how willing God becomes to give away his power to you.

IV

Posture of Defense

...be on the alert. Your adversary, the devil,
prowls about like a roaring lion,
seeking someone to devour.
But resist him...
1 Peter 5:8

Day 18
Defense Adjustment

Need to know

If you recall from the Leadership Edition of *Postured for Power*, as individuals we have much to defend against attack. Add a team to the mix, and the posture of defense takes on an added premium. Greater quantities of assets require broader defenses.

Defense. Make the necessary adjustments to protect what you have built. Don't leave home with out it—you or your team.

Not enough

Is your team stacked with scoring talent? That is good, but not enough! Sports fans know a winning team needs two ingredients: scoring talent and defensive talent. Since points are needed to win, a team that fails to light up the board can expect to lose. But lack of scoring power is not the only way to lose. Without a fortuitous defense, even a talented scoring team winds up on the bottom more often than not.

Almanacs could be filled with stories of losing teams whose offense was good but whose defense was poor. This is true for Kingdom teams of all kinds. Think about failed Kingdom teams you have joined. You look back, take stock of all the talent your team had, and wonder, "What went wrong?

How and why did we fall prey to *that*?"

I'll tell you what went wrong. Your potential was zeroed out because you were poorly equipped in the defense department. The fanciest brochures, the most stunning presentations, the highest batting averages are no substitute for being substantially equipped to route attacks.

What you don't know

The goal of the next several adjustments is to point out some enemies of your team that perhaps you have never thought about, and to help you develop defenses against them. Someone said, "What you don't know can hurt you." How true. Even more true is this statement: What you don't know that you don't know can hurt you worse. It is one thing when something comes out of nowhere, and puts a stranglehold on your team—but you knew it was a possibility. It is quite another when that thing is of a completely foreign species, a creature you never imagined. The suspected surprise is a whammy; but the double unknown is the real killer.

By now you should know the typical enemies of your team. One is a lack of prayer. If the team never prays together, how will it have the mind of God? And how can it expect God to release his power? Another is overt conflict. If the team is at one another's throats consistently, how can it make progress toward a meaningful goal? How can it be productive when its energy is so destructive? Finally, there is the devil himself—plenty of AAA demons included. If he gets the run of the place through a foothold, we all know the result of that.

But what about those adversaries you have never considered? Do you know *all* of your potential predators? Are you sure about that? Sure enough? *Really* sure? We shall see.

Curious?

Now you are probably curious. What dangers could possibly lurk of which I am unaware even exist? Resist the urge to flip to the next page for the answer. That is the wrong thing to do at this moment. The right thing to do is to go straight to the Source.

Yes, pray. Bow your head, fall to your knees, split open those golden-edged pages of your Bible, and begin to seek the wisdom of God. Ask him to reveal to you what you don't know; and to make plain all you don't know that you don't know.

Remember the first humility adjustment? Who is in charge of your team? Do not jump immediately to the words of a stranger. While I believe the following adjustments are based on sound biblical wisdom, what if another danger is more pressing for your team at this hour? Your true Leader knows and wants to share the most current information with you right now.

Do not be unnecessarily spooked. At the same time, the posture of defense is useless if not a ready-posture. It must be attuned to the immediate environment. It must be dialed into the most pressing threats. I can offer you some suggestions, but wouldn't it be a great testimony if you received a word of the Lord about them before flipping the page?

For an author to request his reader to stop reading, you know it must be big. I would that you lay this book aside right now, and request discernment from Heaven. If you will come to him with the right spirit, God will grant you the intelligence you need to discern the greatest threat to your team's existence right now.

Do this first. Pray for wisdom now. Write down what you sense. Get the testimony of two or three witnesses from your team. Begin to draw up plans for defending against the threat or threats God reveals.

Wait until tomorrow to read the next adjustment. Give God a chance to speak *unaided* to you first. Lack of knowledge is the worst enemy facing your team. The way to beat it is getting in the know by getting with God.

God hesitates to grant his power to those who choose ignorance. But to those who choose wisdom, all limits are off. "I am understanding, power is mine" (Pr. 8:14). Is the power yours?

Day 19
Defense Adjustment

Shared Illusion

Ever known someone who seemed to live in a dream world? To them the unreal was real. They seemed to ignore the facts—or they were convinced the facts were in their favor when they were not. You wondered to yourself, "What is so-and-so thinking?" Diagnosis: This person was under an illusion.

Think you are safe from illusions because you are part of a team? Did you know teams are *not* immune to similar illusions? No matter how large or small, every team is prone to shared illusions, and those shared illusions pose a great danger.

To your defenses! Your first hidden enemy is about to be exposed!

Groupthink

The fancy word for shared illusions is "groupthink." A team with groupthink has convinced itself that a particular course of action is absolutely correct, to such a degree that any dissenting facts and/or opinions are not even entertained. (Of that they are entertained with lip service.) Any idea counter to the plan is viewed as moot by virtue of it not being a part of the plan.

Groupthink is really based on feelings more than

accurate thinking. Feelings override sound logic. This sort of team has its mind made up—the trouble is its mind is fixated in the wrong direction.

Before you breathe a sigh of relief because you are too smart for this, you should know that teams with groupthink are not made up of intellectually inferior people. Teams with quite impressive intelligence fall into groupthink. That is how powerful groupthink is. It possesses an undertow powerful enough to suck under all types of people.

Susceptible

In your head you are saying, "Maybe you are susceptible to groupthink, but I am my own person. There is no way *I* would fall to shared illusions." Perhaps some high profile examples will sober you up.

Remember the international cola company that introduced a "new" version of their product back in the 1980's? What a miserable failure! That was a product of groupthink in the organization. They became so enamored with their own ideas that they failed to accurately discern what the public wanted. Dollars untold were lost, and the process of revamping afterward was uphill.

Recall that tragic Space Shuttle re-entry accident in 2003 that took the lives of seven astronauts? That was the product of groupthink within a space agency whose corporate culture glossed over important structural warnings in the craft because the objective of proceeding with another mission was so strong. Even those individuals who afterwards claimed to have sounded pre-flight alarms fell prey to groupthink. If they really felt human lives were in jeopardy, they should have (and could have) done more on the front end of the mission to stop it, even at the risk of their own careers.

More recent to this writing, a major Middle East prison abuse scandal broke news. Troops from the United States subjected prisoners to inexcusably degrading and humiliating treatment. Alone, none of the troops would have committed those atrocities. Together, sealed away in their own world, the shared illusion that such actions were permissible came upon them. And what an illusion it was.

Every team is susceptible to groupthink. Oh yes, even your team. So what if you are "just" a ministry team at your church, or an ad hoc unit at your job. The possibility of duping yourselves into a false sense of reality is real...and can be dangerous.

Aftermath

Groupthink carries an aftermath. All of it. That means it has consequences. One person under an illusion can cause some damage, but an entire delusional team can leave a tornadic trail for the books. Just how widespread that trail becomes depends on the weight and scope of the project. In some cases the aftermath may be nuclear and global; in others it may affect only a tiny circle. Yours likely falls somewhere in between.

Wherever your team falls in the spectrum, get sobered up. Without the proper defenses against groupthink, you very well could bring hurt to real people. A wrong ruling, a faulty decision, a bad acquisition, an off-mark vision, a mis-timed launch—your group may be fully convinced it is on point, and in fact be far off. At worst, people will suffer terribly for your groupthink. At best, your team will experience loss of time and resources, and a major detour after things go south. Is either of these acceptable? If not, take some prevention.

Prevention

Good news! No team is beyond groupthink, but every team can prevent it. Some simple defense postures can head off this complex problem.

First, follow the admonition in the posture of relinquishment to give yourselves ample time to make quality decisions. Avoid the rush. Let ideas sit on the table for a while. Return to them several times. Scrutinize, test, put them through the fire. Entertain all possibilities before acting.

Second, think through the possible consequences of a decision before implementation. If you can live with the consequences (meaning your conscience is clear and your standing before a righteous God will remain good), then you may choose to go for it. I am not saying you should never take risks; just map the bottom as best you can before plunging into the lake. If the consequences would cause guilt, shame, and culpability to fall on your team, you may wish to think again.

Finally, submit major decisions to outside scrutiny. Advisors, coaches, spiritual covering, and the like are invaluable in defending against groupthink. With objectivity of this type in place, you can feel secure that groupthink is a defeated foe.

One enemy down; more to go.

Day 20
Defense Adjustment

Traditionalism

Bold. Maybe a bit brash—like an eager two-year-old thoroughbred huffing and snorting for the Derby gate to open. You are purposeful and driven, with a real sense of "why" you have come together to form a team. You are a team on a mission, and the mission burns in your bones.

Maybe it was to address a social evil, or a new product that needs marketing, or a heroic mission that needs accomplishing. Whatever the reason, when an outsider asks, "Why have you gathered together?" you are able to answer confidently, "Why? Sit for a minute and I'll tell you why...."

This is how the average team begins. A strong start it is. Too bad it is not how the average team ends. Somewhere along the line the *why* fades, the sprawling vine of traditionalism rises up, and the *how* takes over. Order the tombstone now; this once vibrant team is as good as dead.

Defend against traditionalism with all your might!

Mission and method

This is a word about maintaining your mission—which is the why—without becoming too attached to your methodology—which is the how. It is about cultivating flexibility and defending against rigidity.

To be sure, for your team to succeed it will need excellence in both mission and methodology. Mission is the passion side, the fuel. Method is the nuts and bolts part, the implemented strategy for giving feet to the why.

Effective teams have both. A sense of mission saturates every meeting. You remind one another why you are together, why you are dedicated to one another and to the cause. It is through this sense of shared mission that youthfulness flows into the team and pumps it up.

Working hand in hand with the mission is the mechanics. Effective teams are mature enough to know talk is cheap. Doing, not thinking, justifies the team's existence. So you put pen to paper, and then you put that paper to action. You long for the day when you can say "mission accomplished," and you know to get there you have to *get there*.

Trouble creeps in when the embers of mission dim, and the main focus of the team centers on method. Then, with the passage of time in this mindset, the once white-hot mission is forgotten, replaced by a mindset of traditionalism. This is the real danger to defend against.

Traditionalism

Traditionalism is an easy one to spot; but it is not so easy to change. Once it has settled in the only option might be to disband team, much like the only way to eradicate mad cow disease is to burn the carcass. A strong statement, I know. This is why you ought to begin defending against traditionalism beginning at your second meeting!

Traditionalism is set in its ways. It turns up its nose at new methods. Innovation is not just a foreign word; it is a curse word. When challenged on methods, traditionalism retorts, "This is the way we have always done things. It worked in the past, and we believe it will work in the future. If for some reason it fails to work, it is because of other people. Neither our methods nor we are to blame. If people would just get back to the way things used to be, then our methods would work again."

Forgive the childish response to this argument, but duh. Of course your methods would still work if people were the way they used to be. But they aren't! Traditionalism wishes until its dying day for a return to some past glory-days era. You pick it—for one team that era might be the 1950's, while for another it might be last year…or last week.

Cold water

Oh, did that last statement shock you? You thought traditionalism was a problem only for those in their Golden Years, didn't you! Well, it is not.

Here are two maxims you can bank on. *Your team is perilously close to traditionalism every time it meets.* And, the successful team is in more danger of traditionalism than the failed team. Each time your group convenes, the temptation to stick with past methods is strong. This is so particularly for successful teams because, after all, "it" worked in the past so why not use it in the future? Traditionalism is a cliff's edge that you will just have to acknowledge is there, posing a real and present danger around the clock.

Would you like to avoid the cliff? The key is alertness. Teams that slip into groggy and robotic ways of doing business will wander off the edge. Those that remain alert will avoid it. To foster alertness, splash your corporate face with "cold water" questions. If you ask these questions before, during, and after every team initiative, it will have the same effect on the team that cold water has on your physical body. Shock!

First questions: Have we become more focused on the how rather than the why? Why are we doing this? What is our mission anyway? Do we still believe in it? Are we like a thoroughbred that is eager to work, or have we become more like a tired old steed in retirement at a petting zoo?

Second questions: What are some alternative methods for carrying out our mission? Is this the only way of doing things, or can we think of some others? Why don't we try a different method just to stir things up?

Third questions: Does our target group/goal and our method line up? Are we expecting our target to change according to our methods (bad idea), or are we willing to change our methods to achieve the target (good idea)? Is this team made for man, or is man made for this team? (See Mk. 2:27 for the right answer.)

Final questions: Is every method we choose a perfect fit to our mission? Are we undertaking any program or initiative that deviates a single degree from our mission? (Keep in mind, a single degree of deviation between two adjoined lines at the beginning leads to miles of distance at the end all things being equal.)

Ask these questions frequently and ruthlessly. Chill them to as low a temperature as possible so they sting you straight out of your stupor. Do it, and watch power like fresh manna fall from the sky to keep you strong another day.

Day 21
Defense Adjustment

Inner personal

Pop quiz. Think back over the last three days to the threats we have discussed. First was a lack of knowledge, being ignorant of potential threats. Second was shared illusions, the presence of groupthink. Yesterday was traditionalism, focusing on how but forgetting why.

Now for the question: Can you pinpoint the source of these threats? In other words, where do these threats come from?

Got the answer? Read on to see if you are correct.

Inside job

The source of each of the above three threats is the same: internal. That is to say, they are homegrown enemies. Normally, we think of threats as externals. We strap on our binoculars, fire up the radar to scan the distance, and gather intelligence about what *out there* might attack us *in here*. Our eyes are peeled for the Goliath. In the meantime, little foxes sneak in the back door and have the run of the joint.

Our fixation with external dangers is not just a spiritual problem. Did you know that the number one killer of men and women is heart disease? Yet many are more concerned with getting hit by a bus than with paying attention to diet and exercise. Did you know statistically that coastal rip currents take more lives than tornadoes? Or that approximately 7/8 of an iceberg is underneath the water, hidden from sight—and that is the part that brings down a ship?

More teams go down from an inside job than an outside mob. Like heart disease, or a rip current, or a hidden block of ice is lack of knowledge, shared illusions, and focusing on how but forgetting why. All are inner, hidden dangers, easy to neglect until we find ourselves in their unforgiving clutches. The team ignorant to its own self-destructive potential has no one to blame for its collapse but itself!

Mull this over. The truth will set you free. Much like a marriage or family can stand through anything so long as they have one another, so can your team. Nothing on the outside can shake a properly postured group of people. The real enemy is inside troubles caused by you know who. You.

Inner, personal

My apologies if you were hoping for a rally cry against some killer army marching in rank forty deep over the horizon. The threat simply is not that. Remember, the devil prowls, slithers, and squints for tiny footholds (Gen. 3:14; Eph. 4:27). These are his avenues, so we must attend to them first. Engage the enemy where the enemy stands. Dealing with ourselves from an inner, personal angle is the best way, since his first choice is to get at us through us.

Shifting in your seat now? The red dot of the laser pointer is on you. Let's be as truthful as possible without beating a dead horse. Assuming God has called you together, you and your fellow members are the sole determinants of whether you succeed or fail. Not the environment. Not another team. Not illness or tragedy or scarcity of resources. Those will come, to be sure, and they will cause setbacks. Detours are inevitable. Woe to those through whom they come. Yet none of those can be blamed if your team falls apart. Nope, just you.

So many of our *interpersonal* problems have *inner personal* roots. This is not just a cute wordplay. If the team has its head in the sand, the reason might be that the individual members have a spirit of fear. It is always easier to hide behind ignorance. If the team is mired in groupthink, the cause might be personal insecurities amongst the members—a feeling that if I break rank then I will be ostracized. Or if the team is entrenched in traditionalism, or even flirting with it, that might signal stubbornness or pride. These are just some possibilities.

Soul searching

If the call of postured for power is anything, it is one of soul-searching. Three weeks into these adjustments, surely you have figured this out.

Search yourself now. Peer deep inside. Look for inner personal issues that might lead to just the sort of hairline fissures the devil preys upon. Neglect them, and watch the crack in the cement widen into a canyon.

Patch up those fissures. Do what only you can do—change your own ways. Deal with root issues of rebellion, insecurity, arrogance, "my way or the highway" attitudes, and the like. Make yourself as strong as possible for your team.

Then, come together and do the same. By dealing with internal threats, your defenses will become fortified, your team will become impervious, and the power of God will be safe in your capable hands.

Remember, it is not what you know that can hurt you. It is what you do not know that you do not know that delivers the most damaging punch.

V

Posture of Resolution

...firm in your faith, knowing that the same experiences of suffering are being accomplished by your brethren who are in the world.
1 Peter 5:9

Day 22
Resolution Adjustment

Firm up

Toes might get stepped on today as we round the corner to deal with the posture of resolution. Tender hearts might feel a bit chided. This is not intentional; it is just a possibility. We are now to the posture of resolution, which calls for a setting of our faces in a firm direction like a flint.

Our God is strong. He is not weak; neither are his authentic Kingdom teams. A certain sort of steeliness defines the character of highly effective teams. It is this resolute stance that sets them apart for the power of the Almighty God.

Where does your team rank on the firm factor? You are about to find out. The game face is on!

Soft in the middle

Observation: Many of our Kingdom teams are plain soft around the middle. Weak, weak, weak. So pitifully soft.

How so? We are soft on confrontation. We are soft on spiritual disciplines. We are soft on holding one another accountable to follow through with what we said we would do. We are soft when it comes to results. We are soft toward sin.

We are often lazy. As a cover up for our laziness,

we fall back on the sovereignty of God. "If God wants it done, it will get done," we sing, while reclining in our easy chairs. This is what many believers said some centuries ago with respect to world evangelization. And guess what? At a prime moment when missionaries could have shifted the tide around the world, the Christians stayed home.

We have been soft. It is time to firm up!

Firm up

Hands out. Knees bent. Head up. Eyes fixed straight ahead. Firm up that posture in anticipation of the fastball coming blazing down the middle. Grip that bat just right, and let 'er rip!

Firm up, team! Stop talking about unity, and just be unified. Get beyond petty hurts, and get to work. Confront when confrontation is needed. Reward the achievers; warn the underachievers (2 Thess. 3:10-11).

Pay attention to results. Bite your tongue next time you fall back on some old tagline like, "If just one responds it will be worth it." Or, "It's a ministry, so whatever happens happens." Or, "We want to succeed, but not too much." Learn this and learn it well. *He who aims at nothing hits nothing*! Nothing has been our standard as Kingdom teams for way too long. We have been indoctrinated that aiming for something automatically makes us (appear) selfish.

Ha!

What if God took that approach to creation? What if Joshua took that approach in leading the people to the Promised Land? What if Paul took that approach to building the Church? Nothing would be the result. *Nothing*!

For God's sake (literally, for God's sake), perfect pitch after perfect pitch is blazing over the plate. Is there a team out there that can buck up for a minute and knock a few out of the park?

Old fashioned

In these days of nip and tuck solutions to cosmetic appearances, you might hope for such a fix to your team's soft midsection. No such fix exists. If one did, I would do everything in my power to dissuade you from using it. The only sure way to get rid of that unwanted softness is to work hard—the old fashioned way.

The old fashioned way begins with prayer. Lots of it. Church tradition has it that James' knees were calloused from prayer. This type of praying is the type Epaphras demonstrated; it is of the bondslave wrestling type (Col. 4:12).

Another aspect of the old fashioned way includes speaking the truth. Is a member slacking? Is your team faltering and failing? Is the bottom line sagging? Then call it out! Speak the truth. Do so in love; but mince not a single word. Someone has to do it.

Old fashioned needs to become current in these respects. Is the team failing to pay attention to results, and instead eating up minutes dancing around cold realities and basking in the false warmth of brotherly love? You know it cannot last forever. There is a place for fellowship, for friendship, for niceties. But all of the time? Don't you think sometimes it goes overboard?

You know it does. There are times when your team meets and you think silently, "When are we going to get down to business. I appreciate that Terrance is feeling the need to share a personal situation, but does it have to consume thirty minutes of our ninety minute meeting?" Yet you hesitate to voice your opinion for fear of being labeled insensitive by people who would rather hold an inner healing session than put hand to plow.

You have a choice. Risk being labeled insensitive and get done the work God has called you to, or keep stewing white-knuckled in your seat and risk something far worse than the temporary loss of personal reputation.

What could be worse? How about a missed Kingdom moment because your team spent too long in the holy huddle singing camp songs?

Break!

At some point the huddle needs to break. Players must assume their positions. The snap must happen. The action must go into motion. Helmets must crunch. Grass stains and bruises must appear. Someone needs to advance that ball yard upon hard-earned yard until…

Score!

No apologies. Just firm up.

Day 23
Resolution Adjustment
Excellence

Excellence. It should be the minimum standard for every Kingdom team. Unfortunately it is a dirty word in many circles.

Do not let it be a dirty word to you. Get ready to speak a new language than what you might be used to. You have permission to aim as high as you can, with as much ferocious resolution as you can muster. Chin up. The call of the day is to excellence.

A godly standard

Every team has a standard. Yours might be spoken or unspoken, codified or assumed. Nonetheless, your team has a standard of performance that it judges to be acceptable, passable. Typically that standard becomes a baseline for what we will more or less settle. ("Settle." What a terrible word for a Kingdom team!)

What is the standard of your team? While you are pondering that question, let me tell you about the standard of God.

The standard of God is excellence. Of Jesus it is written, "They were utterly astonished, saying, 'He has done all things well; He makes even the deaf to hear and the mute to speak" (Mk. 7:37). Note the sweeping statement, "all things well." What a standard! When he happened upon a blind person, he restored their sight fully. Not half way. Not leaving just a bit of nearsightedness, or just a tinge of blur. Likewise, deaf and mute both could call the day they met Jesus a truly good day. He did more than restore some hearing or a few syllables of speech. When he healed, he pulled out all the stops. Excellence was his way.

What would be the fate of the blind, deaf, or mute if they required the services of your team? Based on your typical accepted performance standards, would they walk away half-healed? Three-quarters well? Ninety-nine parts better? Or one hundred percent restored?!

In other words, what sort of standard does your team typically achieve? Are you mutually satisfied with an ok job? With some flaws but a basically good performance? Or do you aim for the stratosphere every time?

Homework

You have homework. The assignment is something you and your team should have done long ago. Uncap your pens, put on your thinking caps, and write down a clear standard of excellence befitting your team. Ask this question: What does real and true success for us look like? In vivid detail, write down every jot and tittle.

Jot? Tittle? What's that? Historically, those terms refer to the smallest letters of the Hebrew and Greek alphabets. Jot equates with the Hebrew *yhod*, which is essentially a small squiggle the size of an apostrophe ('). Tittle corresponds to the even smaller mark that is the size of the raised dot in the lower case "i."

Recall Jesus' prophecy that, "until heaven and earth pass away, not the smallest letter (jot) or stroke (tittle) shall pass from the Law until it is accomplished" (Matt.5:18). God is so serious about achieving excellence in the Kingdom that he will not permit anything less.

You can't escape. Face it! God is serious about excellence, right down to the last drop. Waste is not in Kingdom vocabulary. Your team needs to buckle into the board table and come up with a definition of excellence that would please God—and then you need to summon the *intentional* resolution to accomplish it.

That Jesus was able to speak so boldly about every jot and tittle coming to pass, and that the sick were made fully well under the hand of Jesus is the result of something called intentionality. Sometimes we might stumble into it. Most of the time, excellence requires volition. Consistent excellence requires consistent intention. It demands a posture of resolution. Please do not expect your team to achieve excellence without resolution. It simply will not happen.

Hence, your homework assignment. What you write will become the standard for the next leg of the race. Be clear. Aim high. Aim right!

Ready, fire, aim!

Let us close today's spiritual workout with a new thought. This might be a bit of a stretch, but let's bring in the concept of sin to the discussion.

Did you know that one Greek word for sin is an

archery term and means, "to miss the mark"? Taken theologically, we sin whenever we miss the mark of God's righteousness. By now we all probably understand this intuitively, and strive as individuals to live uprightly.

Might there also be an application of this particular sin-term to teams? When we miss the mark of team excellence, could it be that we are committing a form of corporate sin? Could it be that we, together, offend the very God whom we are believed to serve when we fire our resources sloppily?

This is uncomfortable to think about because we constantly fight against the concept of a performance-oriented God, in large part to fight legalism in the body of Christ. Taken in the wrong spirit, this surely would lead to legalism. Applied properly, with a mature appraisal of grace, it just might be that spur in our soft bellies we need to get us going again.

(As an aside, think about the mandates of God for the Temple construction. How would he have reacted had the teams involved applied anything less than excellence to that project?)

Take some time with this adjustment. Some real meat hides within these concepts. Legalism can set in. Yet, strangely, I am not concerned about that for you. I am more concerned that you begin aiming higher than you have been. A little voice in my head keeps whispering that God can get more out of your engine—that he can squeeze another drop from your sponge—if your team will just believe it is there.

A higher minimum standard of excellence is possible. Something closer to Jesus' own standard is doable. To settle for anything less is corporate sin. We know that God cannot share his power with those who are in sin.

Day 24
Resolution Adjustment

Confidence

Swagger. Attitude. Poise. Assurance. *Confidence.* Are these good or bad qualities for a Kingdom team? Not only are they good, they are positively indispensable for resolution. Read on.

Indispensable

Can you imagine coffee without the bean? Ice cream without the cream? Rainbow without the green? Neither can I imagine resolution without confidence among the team.

Being postured for power requires all five postures—humility, relinquishment, separation, defense, *and* resolution. Without resolution, which might be defined in one sense as the sheer will to persist, the other postures are for nothing. They are like dynamite minus powder.

In like manner, confidence is an indispensable ingredient to resolution. In the face of challenges, your team needs confidence that it can and will emerge victorious. When the storm clouds build to a menacing formation, your team must be confident that the sun will shine again. Subtract the confidence, and the team will be left like a steak without the meat. It will be a whole lot of nothing.

The trick of it all is to display your confidence in the right way.

Proper display

Confidence comes in two and only two forms: Godly and fleshly. The form your team's confidence assumes has everything to do with everything.

Four times in John's first epistle godly confidence is mentioned. Read for yourself: "Now little children, abide in Him, so that when He appears, we may have confidence and not shrink away from Him in shame at His coming" (1 Jn. 2:28). "Beloved, if our heart does not condemn us, we have confidence before God; and what ever we ask we receive from Him" (3:21-22). "By this, love is perfected with us, so that we may have confidence…because as He is, so also are we in the world" (4:17). "This is the confidence which we have before Him, that, if we ask anything according to His will, He hears us" (5:14).

The third scripture jumps out as particularly important for the resolute confidence of your team: "…because as He is, so also are we in the world" (4:17). Fling open the doors of your spiritual mind and catch the breadth and depth of this revelation! What keys to resolution and power this revelation contains.

This is what our Lord was trying to convey while he was with us in bodily form. Jesus spent himself silly convincing his followers that we would work the works of God, even as he worked the works of God. Candidly, few of God's servants have ever fully latched onto and internalized this truth. John did. I am working on it. Where is your team in the process?

Importance of faith

Confidence so bold comes from one of two places. Either it comes from brash pride, or it comes from humble faith. Be encouraged today to choose the later.

A wise man once said, "Like a bad tooth and an unsteady foot is confidence in a faithless man in time of trouble" (Pr. 25:20). Paul wrote, "Beware of the dogs, beware of the evil workers, beware of the false circumcision; for we are the true circumcision, who worship in the Spirit of God and glory in Christ Jesus and put no confidence in the flesh" (Phil. 3:2-3).

Truly, have confidence. Just be sure your confidence is of the right type, and that it is grounded in faith. Flesh and faith are like oil and water. One must go. Have faith then. Operate from faith. Let faith be upon your team.

Faith in what

First, have faith in God. Confidently believe that he will bring to birth that which he has placed in the womb of your team. Right now, in utter spite of the forecast of man, renew your resolution to push another day. Push that baby out, head, shoulders, and all.

Second, have faith in others. Not everyone is a flake. People may have become a big disappointment to your team. Guess what? Nothing is going to change. The problem with teams is that they are made up of people, and that they have to rely on people to get things done. Yet if your team meetings have become little more than a people-bashing festival, then you are missing the point. You are people too! Take on a new, resolutely confident attitude toward people.

Third, have faith in your collective ability. It might be bottom of the ninth and pulling out a victory may seem impossible. You may have lost ten accounts this quarter, with revenues from your team falling precipitously by the second. People may seem to be running from the help of your ministry team rather than running to receive it. Still, you must not shrink back in your confidence.

Be confident that God hears your prayers. Are you postured properly in the other areas? Is your team pure? Then remember that John teaches you have right standing before God and that he hears you. Be resolute, then, and confident!

Furthermore, be confident that in you reside the collection of talents and gifts necessary to pull off your mission. If self-doubt is hindering to the individual, it is positively paralyzing to a team. Shake off those heavy bands of self-doubt, sound a call to arms, and have everyone take on a renewed sense of ability.

These are practical suggestions. I recently asked each person in our school of leaders to write down his or her strengths and to hand them in to me. Such an exercise is a real confidence builder. You will be amazed—and hopefully invigorated with confidence—at the treasure that lay within.

Confidence. Resolution. They go hand in hand.

"Therefore, do not throw away your confidence, which has a great reward" (Heb. 10:35). A portion of the reward is power to stand resolutely.

Day 25
Resolution Adjustment

Covenant

When you hear the word "covenant," what is your immediate reaction?

The reaction of most postmodern believers is fright and flight. Covenant is synonymous with coffin. It means the personal value of freedom that I hold so dearly is sacrificed.

No such attitude toward covenant ought to be in your team. A corporate resolution to stick it out must be in place. Desertion is not an option.

AWOL

The military has a term for deserters. They are labeled "AWOL," meaning absent without leave. Being absent without leave is a punishable offense, in part because doing so breaks the contract. At a deeper level, it is punishable because it means the soldier has left in the lurch his or her fellow soldiers. Being AWOL in the military is inexcusable.

How much more inexcusable is this action for Kingdom team members! To be absent without leave—which amounts to being absent without love—is a dreadful sin. It signals many deeper issues in the offender that go beyond the scope of this little daily adjustment; but one major issue is a lack of resolution.

Wishy-washy covenant such as this is no covenant at all. Your team cannot survive if the members commit on the surface, yet privately retain the luxury of picking up and moving on should they feel so inclined in the future. This is intolerable!

And it is pervasive. Believers going AWOL is an omnipresent problem. Paul experienced it. "At my first defense no one supported me, but all deserted me" (2 Tim. 4:16). It continues to be a problem in the Church, which accounts for church hopping and high staff turnover. It is a problem in the business community, which accounts for why many business owners and managers have become vocal in recent years about shying away from hiring believers, because non-believers tend to understand loyalty and covenant better. It is also a problem in friendships and marriages, but we will leave that for another book.

Like Paul, I have been deserted many times. One of my key leaders left a voicemail one Sunday morning (at a number he knew I would not be able to answer) that he felt God telling him not to come anymore. Just like that, we were sent into a tailspin from a key wing breaking off to fly alone.

Solutions

Team members who have been on the raw end of a fellow member's untimely decision to walk out on the group are shouting amen right now. You have your own stories to share. Who knows, you yourself may have gone AWOL a time or two.

Your team must become resolute in covenant

with one another. An "I'm not going anywhere" attitude should be upon each member. To date, scientists have not developed a computer chip to make this one happen. God laid down the pattern of covenant, and it is up to each of us to write that pattern on our hearts and put that pattern into resolute practice.

Christ the pattern

Christ is the pattern. He epitomizes covenant. Long before you and I knew it, he entered into a silent covenant with us to seek, save, and walk with us through it all. Jesus overcame temptation (Matt. 4:1-11). He refused distraction (Lk. 9:57-62). He endured anguish—personal from desertion by Judas, physical from crucifixion, and spiritual from separation as the spotless Lamb of God.

To this day through the sacrament of holy communion, also called the Lord's Supper, we remember the covenant of Jesus: "...for this is My blood of the covenant, which is poured out for many for forgiveness of sins" (Matt. 26:28). It is true what Leviticus records, "For the life...is in the blood...for it is the blood by reason of the life that makes atonement" (Lev. 17:11). Through his blood we experienced life.

Life is the point of covenant. To see covenant as a coffin is the mistake of mistakes. Do not be fooled by the postmodern philosophers of the day who campaign for a life free of ties. To drift is to die, because we derive our life through connectedness to others.

We also give life through connectedness to others. This is something the AWOL among us seem to miss. Our strength is the team, not in the individual parts alone. *Stop seeing yourself as the grand asset to the team, and begin seeing the team as an asset to you.*

Christ set the pattern for such covenant. To be sure, he is the greatest asset we could ever have. Even so, he views us as assets to him! This is why he calls us friends and reveals to us his business (Jn. 15:14-15). May we learn a thing or two from our Lord.

Pass it

Let's stop beating around the bush now—enough filibustering of this vote. What are you waiting for? Enter into covenant with the members of your team right now.

You do not even need to wait until the next meeting to pass this resolution. Within the legislative body of your own person, you can push it to a vote and pass it today. This is the beauty of the pattern Christ laid for us. His covenant was a silent covenant, void of bullhorns or skywriting. He made the decision to stick with us, and to this day he has kept that decision solidly.

In the end, that is what really matters. Plenty of people will say they are in the team until the end, only to go AWOL later on. Talk is, as they say, cheap. Quite cheap, in fact. Action counts.

Dream of it. What would it be like to join a team postured with this type of covenantal resolution? Firm up and find out.

VI

Final Push

And after you have suffered a little while,
the God of all grace, who called you to
His eternal glory in Christ, will Himself
perfect, confirm, strengthen, and establish you.
To Him be dominion forever and ever. Amen.
1 Peter 5:9-11

Day 26
Final Push

Humility

Congratulations, you have made it to the final push. The next five days deliver one more adjustment apiece for each of the five postures. Today, humility.

The posture of humility is a downward movement leading to upward mobilization. The upward mobilization part is God's doing. We cannot raise ourselves up any more than we can raise the sun in the morning or the moon at night. If your team is to rise, it must be God who does the elevating.

This speaks to the sovereignty of God. Man is at the mercy of God. Your team is on demand—his demand. His part is to push up as he so will. Your part is to push down.

Push down what? Not what, but whom. You are to push down you.

Push down

You have been programmed from youth to equate one's greatness with one's ability to push up something. A hallmark of physical fitness tests is how many pushups one can do. Most feats of strength involve some form of pushing up. Doubtless it is the word "up" that enthralls us—we always want to go more and higher than the next guy.

Time for some new programming. Your job as a Kingdom team is to leave the "up" to God. Concern yourselves with pushing down.

Carry your cross (Lk. 9:23). Push yourselves down beneath the beam. Be slave of all (Mk. 10:45). Push yourselves down beneath the unlovable and untouchable. Forgive one another (Matt. 18:22). Push yourselves down beneath the pride of holding ill. Posture yourselves under his mighty hand (1 Pet. 5:5-6). Push yourselves under the mighty shadow of the Lord of Hosts.

The real test

Do you possess humility? Let's see if you pass the test. How many "push downs" can you do?

Virtually anyone can do five or ten pushups with good form. Some can do thirty or forty. Very few can do one hundred or more. So it is with spiritual push downs.

Just about anyone can look humble every once in a while by forcing themselves into a posture of humility. Every team has its moments. The test is whether those moments become movements. The real test of humility in your team is whether your posture is more movement than moment.

A spiritual movement occurs at the point where quality and longevity intersect. The team that is able to begin and sustain a downward movement of genuine humility is the one God ultimately empowers. The quality of his empowerment matches the quality of your humility.

He is neither fooled nor impressed by fakery. So

what if you can appear humble for a week or ten days. Maybe you can even pull it off for a month. The Kingdom test requires more. What practical spiritual exercises can your team incorporate to transform your humility moments to a humility movement?

Day 27
Final Push

Relinquishment

Now for a final adjustment of relinquishment. May this adjustment bear the fruit of letting go. Push open the closed that you might fly freely.

Push open

One of the most awesome sights is that of a multitude of doves being simultaneously released. When caged, they are a mere mess of squawking birds. Once released, this breed springs to life with the force and grace of a natural geyser. Picture it.

Your team could be as stunning—except that you remain caged. Stuck in meetings, squawking *ad nauseam* about the same mountainous topic, your team goes nowhere. The force and grace you could be displaying is blocked because you refuse to relinquish certain cares and fears that are doing more harm than help.

I want to see your beauty released; the world needs to see what you can do! Push open the barriers that imprison you. Relinquish the cares and fears that handcuff you to yesterday or to no way. Put some go in your get up. Fly!

The mandate

Don't you know that the collective cares and fears you hold are actually holding you? Each member's refusal to cast it all upon God interweaves with the other members, and they form a chain link cage. Those unrelinquished issues become a web of steely cords the devil uses to ensnare Kingdom teams.

He has you deceived that he created the cage, and that he decides when and if to let you go. He lies. Look closely at the door of the cage. The hinge is weak. The latch is not even in place. A simple push will open your prison right up, and your team can then pour into the air and start reaching those objectives God has placed in your hearts!

Jesus left you the mandate. Your mandate is to fly free. He said, "Go, preach, saying, 'The kingdom of heaven is at hand.' Do not acquire gold, or silver, or copper for your money belts, or a bag for your journey…" (Matt. 10:7,9,10). Leave everything of value behind. Kingdom travel is light.

New values

To this point you have valued some of the wrong things. You have valued past failures and successes above tomorrow's new possibilities. You have valued a hard-nosed stance on a personal opinion more than conceding a point. You have valued a groundless opinion about someone or something, when the facts tell you otherwise. You have valued picking new ideas apart rather than doing new ideas. Relinquish those old values. They weigh you down and hinder your flight. *They imprison you.*

Take on new values. Value possibilities over problems. Treasure the rush of going after the things of God over temporal rewards associated with an unrelinquished grip.

Your observers can't wait to see your beauty. What will it take for your team to relinquish the bags, push open the doors, and fly the coup?

Day 28
Final Push

Separation

Plow up your fallow ground to receive a final adjustment of separation. A harvest of righteous power will result—if you push apart in the right degree and mindset.

Push apart

The theological word for pushing apart or separation is "consecration." It refers to the act of setting oneself apart for a special service unto God. Through consecration we create space for God to live, move, and have his being in our lives.

Scripture commands us: "For I am the Lord your God. Consecrate yourselves therefore, and be holy; for I am holy" (Lev. 11:44). Notice the word "therefore." Someone said whenever you see the word therefore, pause to see what it is there for. In this text, therefore creates an infinite reasoning loop: God is holy, so you must be holy; you must be holy, because God is holy.

Consecration—the posture of separation—is something we do because of the God we serve. He is apart; so we must be apart. Your team must get on his side.

Side decides

The side your team is on decides your measure of godly power. Many times we make the mistake of asking God to get on our side. Our team comes up with some grand idea, and then presents it to God with a "bless this" attitude. Sometimes we do this by accident, with the best of intentions. We present an idea to God and automatically expect that he is going to get behind it because we have done our best.

Not our God. He is the one who said to Joshua, and I paraphrase, "Son, I'm not on your side or their side. I don't choose sides. If you know what's good for you, then you'll get on my side" (cf. Josh. 5:13-15). Needless to say, Joshua complied immediately by falling flat, like a man under the hot pursuit of a police bloodhound.

How is your compliance? When was the last time your team paused for a side check?

Choose

Let's remember one more thing: "You did not choose Me, but I chose you, and appointed you, that you should go and bear fruit, and that your fruit should remain" (Jn. 15:16). He chose your team. He put you together. One of you he called from Illinois, another from Arkansas, another from Chile, and another from Ghana. Each member, born separately and with diverse backgrounds, has been assembled by the edict of God.

On that basis are you to choose him and choose to be separate for him. It is not the other way around. He is not just the reason you decide to become consecrated; he is the reason you can be consecrated in the first place!

With such a terrific concept in view, what side are you consecrated on? What false mindsets might prevent you from pushing apart to choose the one who long ago chose you?

Day 29
Final Push

Defense

Here is a final chance to receive a defense adjustment. There should be no such thing as a defenseless team. You can push back.

Push back

You do not have to lie there and take it limply. If a thief breaks into your house at midnight and threatens your family, you do not have to allow it. If you are wrongfully accused, you do not have to cop to something you did not do. If a bulldozer shows up at your front door and a man informs you without notice that your house is coming down, you do not have to pack right then and leave. You can defend yourself. You can push back.

Does your team have to go under because a few things have come against you? Because a wrench or two has been thrown in to foul up the works? No. You can push back. In fact, you can do one better if you are certain that your destiny is of God. You can flip the script.

The script

Your enemy has a script, and he would like you to become an actor in his grand drama. The script goes something like what Sennacherib delivered by way of messenger to Hezekiah: "Thus says the great king, the king of Assyria, 'What is this confidence that you have? You say (but they are only empty words), 'I have counsel and strength for the war.' Now on whom do you rely, that you have rebelled against me?" (2 Kings 18:19-20).

It is a script of intimidation. The devil's design is to shake you. If he can get you to cave before lifting a finger to fight, he will. You are familiar with this script, because you have read it before. We have all read it before. Now be encouraged to take that script and make it flipped.

Flipped

Your team can flip the script. You can do more than cover your ears and run in the other direction. You can make your enemy read from the same sheet of music he has been pushing on you.

Later in 2 Kings 19:36, scripture records that Sennacherib "departed and returned home." The script was flipped. The mighty ruler of Assyria fled out of fear. Why? How? The secret is found one verse earlier: "Then it happened that night that the angel of the Lord went out, and struck 185,000 in the camp of the Assyrians; and when men rose early in the morning, behold, all of them were dead" (v. 35).

The Lord stepped in on behalf of Hezekiah to defend him, because Hezekiah pushed back in the face of the script. He prayed, "And now, O Lord our God, I pray, deliver us" (19:19). The Lord is your defense. Posture yourself to push back; and watch God go to work. What will it take the enemy's script against your team gets flipped?

Day 30
Final Push

Resolution

Bumped, bruised, and limping, your team drags itself off the field by the scruff of your own necks. You got stomped by the other side. Lost the big contract. Had but a handful show up for a ministry event. Crashed and burned at the moment it seemed to count most. You suffered casualties, real casualties. When time was called, you were at the bottom of the heap. *And you discovered your posture is all wrong.*

Question: Are you sure you read the clock right? What if you misread the clock? You thought final time was called. You thought it's over, and you are washed up for good. But what if it is actually only halftime?

This adjustment is dedicated to everyone—and every team—that has ever wished for a second chance. Push on.

Push on

Every believer and every team need this experience of feeling it is all over, only then to get a second chance. Those familiar with my story know that I burned out badly when I was just twenty-three years of age. I honestly and truly thought my life as a minister of the gospel was over. For a couple of years it basically was, but then God gave me a second chance. He empowered me to push on.

Paul had this experience more than once. He tried and tried to get to his beloved church at Thessalonica. "For we wanted to come to you—I, Paul, more than once—and yet Satan thwarted us" (1 Thess. 2:18). Did he give up though? No, he got creative. First, he sent Timothy. Later, he mailed a couple of letters. Rather than wallowing in the dust, Paul picked up his soul and moved forward. He pushed on.

Have you ever experienced the same? How about your team? Perhaps you have thought collectively that this is it, there is no tomorrow for us. We gave it a shot—our very best shot—but time has been called.

Read this well! Time might not have been called. Do not give up or give in just yet. Now more than ever is the posture of resolution *your* calling. God has more power for you yet. Push on.

Promises, promises

Jesus left us many promises. But I defy you to locate a single promise that this would be easy. While you are searching your concordance in vain, let me share what I read: "In the world you have tribulation..." (Jn. 16:33a).

The promise is a promise of tribulation. It is an interesting word meaning "crushing." That sounds about right for your circumstances, does it not? You feel crushed. Surrounded. You and your team sense the water rising and the walls closing in *all at once.*

Rejoice. If your tribulation comes as a result of

true Kingdom work, then your experience is of the promise!

Second half

There is more. There *is* more. After Jesus tells us our destiny includes tribulation, he includes a second half. He goes on, "...but take courage; I have overcome the world" (16:33b). Can you read this and feel anything less than complete invigoration running straight through your inner man? This song goes out to the beaten down.

As your coach for the past thirty days, let me this chance to speak personally to you one last time. A second half exists.

Take a little time to nurse your wounds. That is natural. Then, get back on that field. Pick up that dropped ball. Resume the race. Run for the prize.

This time, run with resolution energized by courage from the Master. Carry in your bosom an infectious courage. You have been bulldozed. Now, become the bulldozer. He has overcome, so you can overcome. Plow ahead.

Make God proud. Give him reason to point you out in his conversations with the heavenly court. Offer him occasion to gloat with fatherly pride over his children. Allow him the desire of his heart, which is to watch you believing what he said is true. Oh my friends, our Lord longs for ones such as this!

Now to Him who is able to establish you according to my gospel and the preaching of Jesus Christ, according to the revelation of the mystery which has been kept secret for long ages past, but now is manifested, and by the Scriptures of the prophets, according to the commandment of the eternal God, has been made known to all the nations, leading to obedience of faith; to the only wise God, through Jesus Christ, be the glory forever. Amen. (Rom. 16:25-27)

e United States
0001B/51

9 781594 677502